PETE ROSE

BASEBALL'S
CHARLIE HUSTLE

T0117465

PETE ROSE

BASEBALL'S CHARLIE HUSTLE

MIKE TOWLE

Cumberland House
Nashville, Tennessee

Copyright © 2003 by Michael J. Towle

Published by
Cumberland House Publishing, Inc.
431 Harding Industrial Drive
Nashville, TN 37211-3160

All rights reserved. No part of this book may be reproduced or transmitted in any form or by any means, electronic or mechanical, including photocopying and recording, or by any information storage and retrieval system, without permission in writing from the publisher, except for brief quotations in critical reviews and articles.

Cover design: Gore Studio, Inc.
Text design: John Mitchell

Library of Congress Cataloging-in-Publication Data

Towle, Mike.
    Pete Rose : baseball's Charlie Hustle / Mike Towle.
       p. cm.
    Includes bibliographical references and index.
    ISBN 1-58182-353-3 (pbk. paper)
    1. Rose, Pete, 1941-2. Baseball players—United States—Biography.
3. Cincinnati Reds (Baseball team)—History. I. Title.
GV865.R65T69 2003
796.357'092—dc21

                                              2003011130

CONTENTS

—◻︎—

To the true baseball heroes of my youth:
Willie Mays, Sandy Koufax, Carl Yastrzemski,
Tony Conigliaro, and Roberto Clemente

—◻︎—

ACKNOWLEDGMENTS

A work like this involves a lot of research that is possible only with the assistance of others. Rob Butcher and Tina Urban of the Cincinnati Reds and Sina Gabrielli of the Montreal Expos were most helpful in tracking down information and photos crucial to this book. Ditto for Pamela Truesdell, a teacher and advisor to the yearbook staff at Western Hills High School in Cincinnati. Larry Shenk of the Philadelphia Phillies helped by providing telephone numbers.

I am especially grateful to all the people who consented to be interviewed for this book, because there were plenty who were repeatedly approached to no avail. The following gave of their time and memories:

Sparky Anderson, Jack Baldschun, Patricia Blum, Ed Brinkman, Dave Bristol, Bill Conlin, George Culver, John

Dowd, Badger Faison, Ross Grimsley, Bud Harrelson, Richard Hauck, Tommy Helms, Bob Howsam Sr., Charlie Knotts, Bill Lee, Greg Luzinski, Dickie Noles, Jim O'Toole, Jim Phillipps, Mel Queen, John Rewwer, Tracy Ringolsby, Karolyn Rose, Glenn Sample, Eddie Smaldone, Bill Stewart, Tim Sullivan, Pat Thomas, and Jim Wietholter. Bernie Carbo helped with background.

I also leaned heavily on the Internet to dig up much-needed information. One of the best Web sites out there is BaseballLibrary.com. It's a treasure trove of information and trivia.

My comrades at Cumberland House did their thing as the Big Book Machine. Thanks to Ron Pitkin, John Mitchell, Ed Curtis, and Julie Jayne.

My wife, Holley, and son, Andrew, are simply the best. I love you.

I am forever in the service of Jesus Christ, the ultimate safety net for all of eternity. And God bless America.

INTRODUCTION

The Pete Rose Story seeks a happy ending, but that might not be possible in the sense of happily ever after. As this book was being written, Rose remained an outsider, seventeen years removed from his days as a player and still looking for entry into the National Baseball Hall of Fame. Perhaps it is an honor that will never come to Rose, who many believe dishonored the game with his alleged betting on baseball.

Since August 1989, Rose had been serving a life sentence of banishment from the game he lives for. His chance for parole rests in the hands of a Major League Baseball commissioner with problems of his own, starting with an image in need of a P.R. overhaul. These are two downtrodden men in love with a sport that hasn't returned much love lately. Bud Selig sits uneasily in the commish's chair; Pete Rose continues to be spotted in and around casinos. Maybe they can help each other out, Selig by lifting the ban and Pete by pumping some fan enthusiasm back into the game in an official capacity. "Lean on me," they could be saying to each other.

A happy ending for Pete Rose would be a plaque in Cooperstown with his name on it. Or would it? Is that what it would take for Rose to find peace within his soul, to feel complete? Many great baseball players denied a spot in the Hall of Fame have managed to find fulfillment in their post-playing days through other means. Some have achieved restful bliss through the strong bonds of family and rediscovered relationships and/or via the professional stability and sense of achievement offered by a second or third career. Others have made it all the way through self-actualization by the enthusiastic exercise of their faith, making peace with the Almighty.

Where does that leave Pete Rose? What is his fallback? He's now sixty-two years old, with two broken families in tow and another round of tax-evasion charges hanging over his head. As best as can be figured, his second profession is a patchwork of signing shows, memorabilia sales, a few personal appearances here and there, and the occasional work pitching products for companies such as Maaco. Madison Avenue pundits say Rose will make a killing if and when he is reinstated to baseball. That would be good for him, assuming he can avoid the bookies and betting windows while giving to Uncle Sam what is rightfully his.

A lot can be known about a man by how he practices his faith, but that's a great unknown in Rose's life. His first wife, Karolyn, recalls seeing Pete in church only once in her life, and they were married for some fifteen years. That one time was at their Catholic wedding in 1964, during which, halfway through the ceremony and before they had exchanged vows, Pete turned to Karolyn and asked her if they were married yet. If Rose has been inside a church since then to worship, no one seems to know about it. Some who know him would settle for his participation in Gamblers Anonymous, where a twelve-step program that recognizes a higher power could presumably help Rose considerably, but apparently that hasn't yet taken root in his life either.

So that's where we are: watching Pete Rose gaze longingly at Cooperstown from the outside while he wonders what else there is to call his own. All things considered, it would be an injustice if Rose never makes it to Cooperstown in an official capacity. Unofficially, he has been there many times, most notably to set up shop down the street from baseball's holiest shrine during Hall of Fame Week to peddle his autographs and memorabilia. Step right up.

In the pages of this book, veteran *Philadelphia Daily News* sportswriter and columnist Bill Conlin sums up the situation regarding the Hall and Pete quite nicely, saying there has to be a place to put Rose's record-setting 4,256 hits, and that place is Cooperstown. If the Hall of Fame were only about statistics and team achievements, Pete Rose would be a lock. In addition to breaking Ty Cobb's career hits record—along the way notching a record ten seasons of 200 or more hits—Rose also set major-league records for games played (3,562), at-bats (14,053), singles (3,315), total bases by a switch-hitter (5,752), consecutive seasons of 100 or more hits (23), most winning games played in (1,972), and as the only player ever to play at least 500 games at five different positions (first base, second base, third base, left field, and right field). He also played until he was forty-five and ended up with a career batting average of .303, hitting at least .300 in a season as late as age forty (.325 in 1981 while with the Phillies).

Many of the teams Rose played on were champions, or at least winners. While Rose was with the Cincinnati Reds, the Big Red Machine won five divisional titles, four National League pennants, and two World Series championships. He added two National League pennants and a World Series championship while with the Philadelphia Phillies. Then, too, there were the forty-four-game hitting streak in 1978, the Most Valuable Player Award in 1973, the National League's Rookie of the Year Award in 1963, three batting titles, one opposing All-Star catcher flattened, and one take-down of an undersized shortstop in a National League Championship Series.

And to think that most people who knew Pete from his days at Western Hills High School always thought of him as a much better football player than baseball player. Baseball is grateful he picked that route. Pete Rose was a great role model for the game, earning the nickname "Charlie Hustle" from derisive players yet cherishing it as an accurate depic-tion of how he played. He ran out bases on balls, dived head first into bases instead of sliding, stretched singles into dou-bles and doubles into triples, and turned himself into a decent fielder despite below-average hands and a relatively weak arm. He was selected for the National League All-Star team at those five different positions.

Charlie Hustle is a moniker that Rose strived for and earned, and it is one thing that never will be taken away.

PETE ROSE

BASEBALL'S
CHARLIE HUSTLE

1

PEE-WEE PETEY

When we picture Pete Rose at the height of his base-ball career, we see him in the seventies as a cog in the Big Red Machine. Shag haircut similar to Catherine Zeta-Jones in *Chicago*. Beefy, bowed legs, and almost two hundred pounds of supposedly solid bulk packed onto a five-foot-eleven frame. Not real big but certainly no runt.

Vintage Pete Rose circa 1970: Charging around third base and driving a shoulder into Ray Fosse; scuffling at second with scrawny Bud Harrelson; swinging his favorite piece of lumber every chance he could, building up those thick wrists and forearms like no one's business. Not a guy to mess with.

Rose was born tough and aggressive, but he was not born big. *Puny* would be a better word. Not that he was a ninety-eight-pound weakling—just ninety-eight pounds, period, for the longest time. His teammates from Knothole Baseball and schoolmates from Western Hills High School remember young Pete Rose as being smaller than practically all the others boys, and a good many girls, and not even particularly talented when it came to baseball.

Somewhere along the line, someone had the gall to slap the "Pee-Wee" tag on him. More forgiving was a simple "Petey."

Looking at Pete Rose as a fifteen-year-old and again at age thirty, it's hard to believe that he's the same guy from the neck down. From the neck up, it's the same ol' Pete.

⬦

Almost every American metropolis has at least three icons, symbols, and/or slogans that come to mind in describing the city, but Cincinnati, once you get past Pete Rose, is one of the great unknowns. For a few insights into what makes Cincy tick, we turn to longtime resident **"BIG" BILL STAUBITZ,** *a journalist, deputy sheriff, and pro wrestler:*

Cincinnati, as many people know, was very conservative, with a large conservative German population and a large conservative Catholic population. That's not to say nobody knew about sin. They just moved it over the (Ohio) river into the towns of Newport and Covington, Kentucky. You could find nightclubs over there, not too much different from the Las Vegas lounges today. Open gambling. Sports bookmaking. Prostitutes. The syndicates ran the action—this was when Pete was a little kid—it wasn't the healthiest situation. I mean there was all this crapshooting and blackjack and the rest, and ballplayers from one of the National League teams used to go to one of the joints and bet baseball. Not their own games, but their own league, and we don't want that.[1]

⬦

JAMES RESTON JR., author of Collision at Home Plate, *detailing the intersecting lives of Pete Rose and Bart Giamatti, added these insights about Cincinnati and how young Petey fit in:*

Among the German, Polish, and Irish of the riverbank, Pete Rose grew up slowly, little noticed. With his flat, plain, pug-nosed face, and his wide-set eyes, his gapped teeth and freckles, his dime-store clothes, cuffs rolled up on his jeans, there was little to distinguish him from the other children. He was just another river mouse destined to carry on the workingman's tradition. He was small, often smaller than the girls in his grade school and junior high school classes, and had a small boy's cockiness: intent to show he could not be pushed around and ready to fight to prove it. Besides endlessly bouncing a ball off the brick wall of the local tavern, he had almost nothing else in his life, except perhaps collecting pop bottles and camping out on the ridge above the river, stealing the occasional watermelon, and riding the ferry.[2]

"BIG" BILL STAUBITZ was among thousands of Cincinnatians who were exposed to a young Pete Rose:

You have to picture Pete as this bumpy little guy. His family cut his hair—they didn't have fashion styling back then—and Pete's hair stuck up straight. He looked a little bit like a porcupine. He had a gap between his teeth, and he'd spit through it. The way small kids do, he acted tough. But with Pete it wasn't just acting. He was one tough little athlete. Always has been, even though he's not exactly little anymore.[3]

JOHN REWWER, a Cincinnati attorney, grew up with Pete Rose and went to Western Hills High School with the

future baseball star. Rose was slow to mature physically, but even as an undersized youth he had the mannerisms of an ambitious person going somewhere. Rewwer:

The first time I ever saw Pete was in Knothole Baseball (Cincinnati's equivalent to Little League), where I played against him. Even back in those days he had this certain flair about him, even though he wasn't someone you would say had superior talent. His talent just had to catch up with him. But he had this great self-confidence. He stood out from the rest, and he was the first switch-hitter I ever saw in my life.

I'll never forget walking past the stands at a local ball-park one day and overhearing a couple of men say, "That kid is going to be in the major leagues someday."

Pete never really excelled—he was flashy and every-thing—but he was no Eddie Brinkman growing up. Eddie was a natural, where Pete worked hard, although he did have the major-league moves. Actually, he was a much better football player in high school, a Jimmy Brown-type of runner, than he was a baseball player. There would be five or six guys converging on him, then he would squirt loose and run for another five or ten yards. He was just a real hard guy to tackle.

I wouldn't say Pete was a runt as a kid, but he wasn't a big, strong guy either. He just wanted to play, and he played hard.

*If Pete Rose as a kid was the ugly duckling who wouldn't blossom until after high school, classmate **EDDIE BRINKMAN** was the area's can't-miss prospect— a lanky, well-rounded athlete with fluid moves who excelled at both basketball and baseball. Brinkman:*

I'm eight months younger than Pete. He was born in April and I was born in December, the day after the attack on Pearl Harbor.

Pete and I became pretty good friends starting in high school. We grew up about a mile apart, but somewhere in that mile was the dividing line for schools, which is why I didn't really get to know him until we were teenagers. He went to elementary and junior high school out west of where I did.

Starting at about age nine or ten, we played Knothole ball together. It was Class-C Knothole. I was small myself at the time, but Pete was really tiny, even

WESTERN HILLS HIGH SCHOOL ANNUAL PHOTO

At Western Hills High, Pete Rose was known more for his football prowess than his baseball skills. He was a fearless, Jim Brown-type running back with a knack for squirting out of pileups to ramble for additional yardage.

smaller than me. That was my first year of playing organized baseball of any kind. Pete was the catcher, and I think he caught because he could catch the ball. Besides, I don't think anyone else wanted to put the catcher's gear on. I played mostly outfield—they put me someplace where I couldn't hurt anybody.

We didn't have a very good team. We had a bunch of kids from down along the river—they called us "river rats." We had just enough kids to field a team, really. Pete's father was a bank teller and my dad was a factory worker, so we were what you might consider low middle class or upper poor, I'm not sure which. Whatever it was, neither of us really had that much.

We played together about three or four years. Once we got to Class-A Knothole, they had to disband the team because we didn't have enough kids to play. I guess when you get to be fourteen or fifteen years old, guys have other things on their plates: maybe girlfriends, maybe wanting to get a job in the summer.

So Pete and I—we called it going up the hill—went up and got onto an A team up there, although on different teams. Even then, we really didn't have a clue at the time as to how far we might go in baseball because it's not like we had been seen by any scouts. We were just playing and enjoying ourselves, having fun.

Another high school acquaintance was JIM PHILLIPPS, who saw Rose's pedigree as something that would go a long way in shaping the youngster who would later become known as Charlie Hustle, and would bowl over catchers and scrape with opposing infielders:

Pete came from a part of town, Sedamsville, where you couldn't afford to be a mousy guy. There were some tough guys from that neighborhood, and you didn't want to get into a fight with them. Some of the guys who came from that area were really good athletes. Don Zimmer, for one.

Rose grew up in a household with a tough, jock-minded dad, Harry Rose, who was somewhat of an athletic legend around town, playing semipro football well into his forties. LAVERNE NOETH, Pete's mom, reflects:

His daddy never let up on Peter. If Peter got four hits and he came home with a smile on his face, his daddy would want to know about the time at bat he didn't get a hit. And if, God forbid, his daddy ever saw that he wasn't hustling, he would really let him have it.

Did Peter ever mind? Maybe sometimes he would feel disappointed that his daddy didn't praise him without always including a lesson. But he didn't show it. I don't think he got upset, because he wanted the exact same thing his daddy wanted for him. He wanted to be a pro player.[4]

Few people know the history of baseball in and around Cincinnati as well as **GLENN SAMPLE** *does. A few years older than Pete, he grew up not far from where Rose did, went to the University of Cincinnati on a baseball-football scholarship, later coached the Bearcats in baseball, and for many years has been the official scorer at Reds' home games. Sample:*

I lived in Price Hill, about five miles from where Pete grew up, in Sedamsville. I was ten years older than Pete, and one of my best friends was Don Zimmer, who also grew up nearby. And it was mainly because I spent a lot of time with Don Zimmer that I got to know Pete. I also used to play ball against Pete's dad.

Pete was the peppery little guy who had a reputation for his great enthusiasm. As far as mechanics go, he wasn't that great a ballplayer. Yet he was a winner.

When he was growing up, Pete was a real little guy. Zimmer was pretty small, too. I think he was about five-six and ninety-eight pounds when he was playing high school ball.

Although Pete started out as a catcher in Knothole ball, he was moved to second base by the time he got to high school. I saw him play a few games. He didn't have the greatest arm and wasn't that good a fielder, but he was a pretty good hitter. He'd hit line drives and ground balls through the infield, but nothing much more than that. They weren't exactly rockets.

One thing you would notice about him was how he would run hard, back out into the field, right after his team had made the third out while batting. When the other team made the third out in their half of the inning, Pete would sprint back to the bench, and there he would always be swinging a bat. This is the way it was, inning after inning after inning.

⚏

Another Cincinnati legend was **PAUL "PAPPY" NOHR**, *for many years head baseball coach at Western Hills:*

When Pete came to school he was a little fellow, and he wanted to play catcher. Now, we had a good catcher, big guy, name escapes me, so we put Pete at second base. Pete wasn't the greatest infielder, but he was learning a new position. He began as a backup. Just a little kid with stiff hair. We all knew his dad played pretty rough football.

Young Pete was a hard worker, but he never did win honors for high school baseball. Good bunter. Ran hard. Ran out everything. But he wasn't the fastest guy on the team. Attitude, that's what they talk about now, isn't it? The kid had a great attitude.[5]

⚏

CHIP "BADGER" FAISON, also a Western Hills alum close to Rose in age, adds some background about Western Hills and Pete's years there. Even though Faison lived outside the school's zone, he was permitted to go there by paying tuition:

I really wanted to go there because I knew it was a great sports school. We didn't have a lot of black kids in school— maybe four in the whole school back then. One of the other big schools was Purcell, which is where Roger Staubach went to school. Roger was the All-American guy, the well-known sports star in high school and prom king who went on to the Naval Academy and eventually married his high school sweetheart. Pete, who I think was the same age as Roger, was none of that.

Pete was always hustling, even in high school. He was Charlie Hustle before he was (actually known as) Charlie Hustle. In football he would always run back to the huddle after a play, and in baseball he was always running hard around the bases. In that way he was nothing like Junior (Cincinnati Reds superstar Ken Griffey Jr.) who would take a big swing, hit a drive, and stand there at the plate watching the ball. As soon as Pete swung and made contact, he was immediately off and running full steam. As far as that goes, whenever it was time for players to run somewhere, Pete would be the first one to take off and get there.

I can still visualize Pete running the ball in football. He was fast, agile, and quick. He would take stutter steps to avoid getting tackled, and he was great at zigzagging in and out around guys. He was an exciting runner, fun to watch.

Former Reds scout CHARLIE KNOTTS has known Rose almost fifty years:

There's no way that Pete Rose ever bet against the Reds. He's too much of a competitor for that. Pete Rose is Cincinnati. He is the most-loved man in the city. Pete might be difficult to like, but what he accomplished was so exciting. That was the big thing.

He certainly wasn't super talented. I saw a scouting report on him once: can't run, can't throw, can't hit. I about

WESTERN HILLS HIGH SCHOOL ANNUAL PHOTO

Star running back Pete Rose, Number 55 in the front row, poses for a yearbook photo with other members of the Western Hills High football team.

crapped when I saw that—I think it was filed when he was playing for that minor-league team in (Geneva) New York. I do know that the worst thing about Pete was his arm. He wasn't a great fielder either, but he would let the ball hit him in the mouth before he'd let it get away from him.

I saw Pete play high school ball, amateur ball, and pro ball—I watched him play it all. It's hard to say who was the greatest baseball player of all time, but in terms of players accomplishing their goals, I would have to say that Pete Rose was the greatest. He didn't have the power of Mickey Mantle; he didn't have the talent of Stan Musial. Everything he did, he did out of guts and hard work. He always played the same regardless of the weather—whether it was warm and sunny or rainy and cold. He was running out walks long before he got to the pros.

In the wintertime Pete would hang his ball glove on the handlebars of his bicycle and ride around, looking for anybody to play toss with him. He didn't care how cold it was.

He's one of the fiercest competitors I've ever seen in my life. I've never seen anything like it, and he's never looked over his shoulder.

You know, his dad wouldn't let him play ball for any team unless they let him switch-hit. His dad was a semipro football player. Pete was a heckuva football player himself, but he's lucky he stuck with baseball, because he became very famous for playing it and made a good living with it. Baseball was Pete's game.

JIM WIETHOLTER *is a year younger than Rose but caught up to Charlie Hustle in school when Rose repeated his sophomore year:*

Nobody ever accused Pete Rose of being smart. As the luck of the draw would have it, in his second sophomore year, I got assigned into the same health class that he was in. We were once assigned to do a paper on the Cincinnati city water works together. Guess what? I ended up doing the project myself, and it ended up being what might have been one of the few A's Pete ever got in high school. I don't know that as a fact, but I do know that on that project he did very little, if any, of the work.

To do the project research, I got ahold of a lot of the handouts and pamphlets from the city. I also made a trip down to one of the treatment stations, and then on to one of the new sewage-treatment stations, which was a new thing in those days. It took some effort for what might have been a two-page paper, but you had to do a little bit of legwork. There was no Internet in those days; what you had was the encyclopedia in the library. If you were really lucky and your family was rich, you might have an encyclopedia at home. So it took some work on my part, and I can tell you I'm pretty certain that Pete didn't even read our paper before it got turned in.

*JIM PHILLIPPS offers another look back at the Rose era
at Western Hills High School, with a focus on football:*

I remember him mostly in high school as a football player.
Pete has a lot of his dad in him. Harry had a reputation
around Cincinnati for being one heck of an athlete, especially
in semipro football. Pete also was an outstanding football
player, and no doubt he was the best player on the team. Very
shifty and followed his linemen very well. He didn't need a
good, clean block to get going. All he needed was a lineman
or another back to get between him and a would-be tackler,
and Pete could juke his way around for some nice gains.

I remember him playing a game against Hamilton
Public, which is a sort of football power up here in south-
western Ohio, and his carrying a couple of guys on his back
on a key play.

I actually got to know him better later in life because my
kids went to high school with his children. My son, Jerrod,
played on a basketball team with young Pete, and I coached
a Knothole League team that competed against young Pete.
Whenever I was around Pete, he was a nice guy, very friendly.

*If Rose was one of Western Hills' big-name football
players, fellow future major-leaguer Eddie Brinkman
was the school's biggest baseball star. GLENN SAMPLE:*

Ed was head and shoulders above Pete in high school in
terms of baseball ability. Ed hit the long ball, had a good arm,
and was an outstanding defensive guy—he had more of the
things that major-league scouts were looking for. That's how
he got a nice signing bonus from the (Washington) Senators.

Ed had a great career in the majors, although he had
trouble hitting. Pete, on the other hand, was the type of guy
who got better every year. In all my years of coaching,

including thirty years at the University of Cincinnati, both baseball and football, I would see guys eighteen, nineteen years old, who had been great high school stars, but they never got any better. Pete was the antithesis to that. He was one of those other kids who just started getting better at age eighteen.

***ED BRINKMAN** gives this explanation for why he thinks he got to the majors quicker than Rose did:*

I don't really know what it was the scouts saw in me. I wish I knew. For one thing, I was always very skinny, real skinny. During my big-league days, I was known as a defensive guy, and people would ask me questions about how good I was. I said, "I don't know; I never saw myself play." If you don't see yourself, there's really no way to know. But I was told I had a great arm.

There are certain things you can't teach, and arm strength is one. I was also told I had pretty good instincts for the game. That's another thing that scouts look for that can't be taught. A guy just needs to know what to do in certain situations. That's really the only reason I can think of as to why they might have watched me more than Pete.

What's important to remember is that I had a chance to play on some teams that played in some national tournaments. I also remember playing on a team in 1959 that went to a big tournament in Altoona, Pennsylvania, and Roger Staubach was on a team. He played center field on that team. I was fortunate to play on some teams or against teams with some really good players on them, and scouts would come out to watch those guys. I got noticed because of all the other good players on the teams I played on.

BRINKMAN *elaborates on Western Hills:*

We had a great tradition. Cincinnati was a big baseball city, and all the kids in the city played baseball at that time. Now they've got so many other things they can do, but in those days we didn't really have anything else to do. We played baseball all day, every day, in our neighborhoods.

Pappy Nohr was a great coach because he taught fundamentals so well. Besides the physical abilities, like throwing and hitting, he spent a lot of time teaching about other fundamentals, like how to bunt.

Pete was still very tiny in high school. In those days there was no draft—everybody was a free agent—so you could sign with anybody. When Pete graduated in June 1960, I don't think any team wanted to sign him.

What helped my cause coming out of school is that I had played on an American Legion team that won the national championship. We had a lot of good players on that team, and several of those guys signed, although I don't think any of those other guys ever made it to the majors. Pete wasn't on that team.

The scouts came to the finals of the American Legion playoffs. We won the state championship in Columbus (Ohio), along the way beating the team Pete played on, then we went to the state and won there, then Richmond, Indiana, for a regional tournament, then a place called Hobart, Oklahoma, for a sectional tournament, and then, finally, Colorado Springs for the finals. Every place we went there were a lot of scouts to watch us.

We just had a really good team and everyone contributed. That's when I first caught the scouts' eye. Then I had another year or two of high school eligibility left, and scouts started coming to see me play high school ball. On the other hand, Pete's American Legion team didn't go that far, so the scouts never really zeroed in on him.

WESTERN HILLS HIGH SCHOOL ANNUAL PHOTO

This Western Hills team photo shows Pete in back row, second from left. Fellow future major-leaguer Ed Brinkman is in the front row, far left.

Pete Rose is a tough guy. He played tough in football, was a tough out in baseball, and had a tough time the one occasion he stepped into a boxing ring. Three days shy of his sixteenth birthday, on April 11, 1957, Rose fought an opponent named Virgil Cole in a 112-pound bout. This is what ROGER KAHN wrote in the autobiography on which he collaborated with Rose:

Virgil Cole was more experienced and unawed by his peppery opponent. He pounded Pete hard in the body and face. Pete's own punches, when he got any off, were wild. Mostly his role in the fight turned out to be target.

During the second round Pete's sister Caryl cried out, "Dad, can't you stop it? They're beating his brains out. They're killing him."

Harry Rose said, "He's all right. He's not getting hurt. He knows how to defend himself." But as the beating continued, Harry's eyes grew wet.

Pete stayed dry-eyed and on his feet, but lost the decision by a wide margin. When the family returned to the Braddock

Avenue house, Pete wore his bruises like medals. "Look at me," he told his mother. "But he couldn't knock me out."[6]

⊏◊⊐

BADGER FAISON, who played some football and was on the swimming team at Western Hills, also has some memories of Pete Rose away from the athletic field. Faison offers some scattershot memories:

Pete wasn't Mr. Popular, and I don't remember him dating girls, although he probably did, even though I don't remember seeing him at dances.

Fraternities were big in our high school then, and to the best of my knowledge, he didn't belong to one.

I don't remember Pete as a loud kind of guy; he was kind of low profile. Pete wasn't a real team guy either, at least not in the sense of one of those who would chum around other guys or slap them on the back for a good play.

In high school you have groups like the nerds, the eggheads, the jocks, and the greasers, and I don't remember Pete as being in any of those groups.

It was a different kind of era. There was a strong work ethic, and most of the guys who played sports were pretty much straight arrows. Nobody smoked, nobody drank, and there was never any drugs. But we all liked girls, cars, and sports. Those were the big things. Cruising was part of the scene at the time, too.

⊏◊⊐

RALPH GRIESSER played quarterback at Western Hills and went on to play football at the University of Michigan:

Pete had his scrapes, but he was not a kid who got in that much trouble. Maybe he appeared to others as a dead-end kid, because that was his look. But I don't think anyone considered him a problem, other than academically. He had a few borderline friends from the neighborhood, but he also had friends who were solid people. One of his friends became a high school principal and another became a priest. How bad were those guys?[7]

⬦

GRIESSER offers this assessment of Rose's football skills:

Pete was very small, but quick. He would do things like you would see on the cartoons—disappear into the pile and come out on the other side. Even on film, you couldn't tell how he did it. He was very competitive, very tough, and had great hands. I would throw him little dump passes and away he would go, without blocking. He put on a show one game. We beat a team, 60–6, and he gained some phenomenal amount of yards and scored a bunch of touchdowns.[8]

⬦

Adds GRIESSER:

In my senior year Pete was five-foot-eight. A developing kid. He tried out for quarterback, halfback, and everywhere on defense. In the end we moved Charlie Scott, a good halfback who went on to West Point, to fullback, and we played Pete at half. Pete was one fine receiver coming out of the back-field. He must have gained four hundred yards receiving and another six hundred running the ball. He also kicked our extra points and some field goals. . . .

Pete had a lot of the same characteristics in football that he later showed in baseball. Competitive. Tough. No super speed, but excellent quickness. But as a young man Pete was no phe-nom. College recruiters came to see us, and they rated six or seven others ahead of Pete. His biggest qualities were not overpowering skills. But he didn't back away from any man or any thing.[9]

◆

People often credit Harry Rose for his son's competitive foundation, but Pete's mom also was a big influence. LAVERNE NOETH, Pete's mother, remarried after Harry's death in 1970. Noeth:

I didn't take nothing from nobody. I wouldn't stand back from a fight. A couple of times I pulled a girl out of a bar and whooped the hell out of her. One time, I was already married. I was in my mid-twenties, and I already had a couple of kids. She was telling somebody I was running around with her husband. I went right in the Trolley Tavern and I dragged her out, and I knocked the living hell out of her. We were real, real good friends. I don't know why she ever started something like that, but I just went in and grabbed her.[10]

◆

One of Rose's most memorable plays in football became a highlight reel in Western Hills' archive, as former high school football teammate JIM WIETHOLTER recalls:

I remember seeing game film of this one time when we played Central High School, which at the time was public school champs. On one play, Pete went something like thirty-five yards for a touchdown, which doesn't sound like a particularly great accomplishment, except that he had lost his helmet, had his jersey torn, and had at least two guys holding onto him as he went over the goal line. And if you look closely at the whole play, you can see that all eleven players on defense touched him at one time or another during that run. Unbelievable, although I guess it shows that the rest of us weren't doing too much to help him.

WIETHOLTER:

WESTERN HILLS HIGH SCHOOL ANNUAL PHOTO

The thing about Pete was that he wasn't a big guy until his senior year, and even then he might have been about five-foot-nine and 160 pounds. The inside dope on him was that if you got in a fight

Western Hills scatback Pete Rose finally is brought to the ground after rushing for a nice gain.

with him, you had better kill him because that was the only way he was going to quit.

Mostly because of his football exploits, Rose became fairly well known around the Western Hills campus. Underclassmen looked up to him, at least in terms of his athletic abilities. One of those underclassmen was **PAT THOMAS**, who still works at Western Hills in student discipline and helps coach the girls softball team:

I'm about three years younger than Pete and first learned about him when I went out for freshman football, and they showed us that highlight film of the play in which Pete ran for a touchdown despite getting touched by at least ten members of the other team. They showed us the clip as a motivational thing to get us fired up for football, and it was effective. It made a spectacular impression on me.

I also remember that he had a girlfriend who was a year older than me, and I was in a class or two with her. I would see Pete walking her to class, and I remember thinking how cool it was—to see in person the same Pete Rose I had been in awe of on the football film. I did get to talk to him a little bit, but back then there was something of a respect barrier, in which kids rarely talked to upperclassmen, especially ones three years older.

Pete was kind of cool in high school, too. Not Fonzie kind of cool, but definitely like one of the cooler guys. I guess he was more mature than other kids his age, so he carried himself more responsibly than a lot of guys.

THOMAS gives some added background about what it was like to grow up on the West Side of Cincinnati:

I've been a West Sider all my life, dyed in the wool. I get nervous if I go on the other side of Vine Street—that's the street down the middle of Cincinnati. There are some West Siders, I'm sure, who would disagree with this, but I'm sure most West Siders for years have believed that the sun rose and set on Pete Rose. He was held in extremely high esteem.

I have a theory that the West Side of town developed more as kind of a working-class part of town. Much of the older money in town went to places like Mount Lookout, Hyde Park, Mount Washington, and Lynnwood. Those places are all on the East Side. Don't get me wrong—I have good friends that live on the East Side of town. But West Siders tend to want to do business in their neighborhood and keep things at home. The more flashy, yuppie lifestyle is on the East Side.

West Siders are a little more down to earth. *Plainer* might be the right word. Pete epitomized the West Side. He grew up in Sedamsville, which is down near what used to be known as Boldface Park. It's now called Pete Rose Park, at the corner of Fairbanks and U.S. 50.

-¤-

JIM WIETHOLTER:

One thing you need to remember about Western Hills during the days when Rose was there, is that it wasn't just a high school, it also was a junior high. You had seventh through twelfth grade and something like three thousand students all in the same building. It was a collector high school for all of those area county school districts that didn't have their own high school, so you had people coming from all over the city. It was a big melting pot beginning in the ninth grade, although a lot of us already knew each other from having played sports against one another.

Between freshman and senior year, our class was weeded down from about 760 students to 570 by the time we graduated, and in that day that was a humongous graduating class. I suppose there were people who felt like they got lost in the school, but I never felt that way. Everyone seemed to have a group of friends they could call their own. I don't remember there being any outcasts. If there were any, say, nerds, they had their group. Some of the students were stupendous—two of the kids in our class got perfect eight hundreds in both English and math on their SATs.

Ethnically, we were not very diverse. In our graduating class, there was one black girl. We had fraternities and sororities. That's where the in-groups were. But there were other groups that crossed group lines, like a Hi-Y thing that went on every Tuesday night. That was a mixing group that had jocks and nonjocks, and smart guys and dumb guys, and everyone just kind of got together there.

-¤-

*JIM PHILLIPPS offers this quick take on another aspect
of high school life at Western Hills, circa 1960:*

Cincinnati is a pretty conservative town. When we were in
high school, it was considered a big deal to get our hands on
a couple of bottles of beer or a bottle of wine. And the
biggest disruption we had in the classroom was the occasional eraser fight.

*JIM WIETHOLTER got plenty of chances to run into
Pete on the field, both in football and baseball. He
recalls some of those encounters:*

Pete Rose was a tough dude, and even though he wasn't a
great player, you knew that trying out for baseball he would
make the team. The first time I went to bat in the gym, he
was tossing batting practice. That sucker threw this big
damn ol' curveball right over my hands and made me look
dumb as hell, and I'll never forgive him for that.

Then our senior year he came out during summer practice in football, and he was with some of the older guys
who would come back and give us younger guys some
insights as to how to make a downfield block and other
things like that. He was fairly helpful. One of the things
Pete liked to do more than anything else concerned this
drill in which the linemen got to carry the ball. Pete always
wanted to be in on the stop so he could tackle some of us
linemen. He would just put his head down and crash helmets with you.

*PAT THOMAS also remembers Rose as someone who
would sometimes come out for practices to help out,
even after he had played out his eligibility:*

I took some infield practice with him, as I was a first baseman. He was already out of school at the time, and he
would sometimes come back to help out for a few days. In
just the year or so that he had been out of high school,
something with him had changed. He was bigger, stronger.
During infield practice, he was taking some grounders at
second and relaying to me on double plays, and that ball
was coming to me about twice as hard as anyone had ever
thrown to me before. And he wasn't supposed to have a
great arm? I'll never forget that. *Whaaaccckkk!!* Damn,
that hurt.

One of my favorite reminders about Western Hills
baseball from that era is a picture in the annual that shows
Pete covering second base with a guy sliding in. That other
guy happens to be Eddie Brinkman. It makes me wonder if
there is any other high school annual in America that
shows two future major-leaguers back when they were
high school teammates involved in the same play, even if
just practice. Just out of curiosity, I called around to a couple of collectors to see what kind of money that annual
with the photo would bring. They said something like fifty
bucks. I don't know about that. I think it's worth a lot more
than that.

By the way, some of the other Western Hills alumni who
went on to success in the pros were Jim Frey, Chuck
Brinkman, Ed Brinkman, Don Zimmer, Clyde Vollmer, Dick
Drott, Art Mahaffey, Russ Nixon, and Herman Wehmeier, as
well as Jack Reynolds, who would play football with the Los
Angeles Rams.

*RICHARD HAUCK, now retired, still lives in the West
Side of Cincinnati, just minutes from Western Hills,
where for many years he coached sports, first as a
"reserve coach" under Pappy Nohr, before taking over*

the baseball program in 1963. Hauck recalls what
baseball practice was like in those days:

Our baseball practices were short, and everyone stayed busy.
Nobody stood around. That was also true for the managers,
who would help out in batting practice or hitting balls to the
guys in the field. Practices were an hour and a half, and that
was it. Then we quit.

Before practice, I would make out a personalized list for
each ballplayer showing him his shortcomings and what he
needed to work on. I would allot fifteen minutes for that
individual work in the middle of practice. My philosophy
always was to work on the things that very seldom happened, the unexpected. Most baseball players can make your
average play, but the good team had to be prepared to make
the play that might come only once a season. We worked
more on the difficult things than we did the normal things.
That's how we kept improving.

Sometimes, when the Reds were playing night games,
Pete would come by and participate in our practices. He
would take some ground balls, step in to do some hitting, and
take some time to talk to the ballplayers. Across the field you
might see the track team out working out. Pete would say, "I
can beat those guys," and so he would leave the ballfield and
go over there and run the hundred-yard dash with those guys.

The guys thought it was great having Pete around the
ballfield, and he was terrific. He was a good guy, very con-
genial and very likable. He talked to everybody, and all kinds
of confidence rubbed off on us.

Pete made himself into a ballplayer, and he was a great
one. In high school, though, Eddie Brinkman had it all over
him. Coming out of high school, Eddie would cash his
checks at the bank and Pete would cash his at the drugstore.

-=I0I=-

***HAUCK* continues:**

Pete was a good football player, a halfback. He could have gone to Miami University (Ohio) and played there. He wasn't blindingly fast, but he was determined. He wouldn't quit. Sometimes he would go into a pileup and then pop out, and you had no clue as to how he was able to do it.

WESTERN HILLS HIGH SCHOOL ANNUAL PHOTO

In practice, Rose goes to first with the throw while Western Hills teammate Ed Brinkman slides into second.

Pete's strong point was his desire to excel at whatever he did. Obviously, that same desire wasn't there in the classroom. He did just enough to get by. But he's gotta be smart. I mean, he can rattle off statistics, and he can tell you about trivial things years after they happened. If he had really applied his mind in the classroom, I'm sure he would have been just as successful there. But he didn't.

Sports was the only thing on his mind. School to him was merely a vehicle that allowed him to play sports.

JIM WIETHOLTER* *was among many constantly reminded of how dedicated Rose was in trying to overcome a dearth of talent that perhaps only he was oblivious to:

Pete didn't really stand out in any way. He was a tough guy whose dad would often show up to watch him in morning practices. Usually, Mr. Rose was the only dad there. That was a positive. And Rose had desire. He wasn't that fast, couldn't hit the long ball very well, had an average arm, and was a mediocre fielder. So what have you got? You've got a guy who taught himself, as how to hit left-handed and right-handed.

Down on Ferguson Drive there was a place they used to call the trampoline center. That's where they had trampolines in the ground, and you could pay a fee and go in there and jump on them. They also had batting cages with automatic pitching machines. I'd see Pete stand in there and hit against one of those machines for hours, practicing left-handed and right-handed.

PATRICIA BLUM went to Western Hills, and that's where she met her future husband, Ed, who would get to know Rose from playing on a men's football team with him. Ed Blum and Rose were in the same graduating class of 1960, although it's hard to believe that Pete actually was a part of the school scene during the 1959–60 school year. He had used up his sports eligibility after repeating his sophomore year. There is no senior picture of Rose in the school's 1960 annual. A careful page-by-page look at that thick 1960 yearbook turns up only one tiny photo of Rose, his head barely visible between shoulders, with him standing in the back row of a group of about eighty members of the Maroon W Club. The photo is on page 162, a number which should be of obvious interest to a statistical nut with Rose's baseball IQ. Patricia Blum:

My husband, Ed, was in the same graduating class as Pete, 1960, and I'm not sure if Pete ever actually graduated. I can remember going to the graduation ceremony and don't remember seeing Pete there. Pete wasn't the sharpest tool in the shed.

〜〜〜

PATRICIA BLUM *continues:*

I knew Pete, but not as well as my husband, Ed, knew him. They played football together in a Sunday afternoon league in the fall of 1959. Their team was the Grosbeck Green Devils.

My funniest memory of Pete is the car story. Ed had this car, and I thought it was ancient. In fact, it *was* ancient. It was a '37 Plymouth coupe. Ed had had it when he and I first started dating, and I hated that car because there wasn't enough room in it for anyone but the two of us.

I think I nagged Ed enough about the car. Pete was nagging him about it, too, for a different reason. Pete needed a car and wanted to buy Ed's car in the worst way. Finally, I told Ed to go ahead and get rid of it, although now when I think about it, that car would be worth a fortune today. It was in mint condition, but I wanted something like a convertible, with room enough for more than two people.

Pete bought it. I remember that Pete's mom knew Ed's mom quite well. After Pete bought the car, his mom called my future mother-in-law and just raised a terrible ruckus with her because Pete couldn't afford it. A second reason was that there wasn't enough room in that car for Pete to take his mother to the grocery store. Her concern was that her Petey wouldn't be able to get her and her groceries into that car.

Ed's mom told her that it was out of her hands, that Pete had bought the car and it now belonged to him. A deal's a deal. It wasn't any time later that the Reds signed Pete, and he went out and immediately bought a Corvette. I don't know what happened to the Plymouth coupe. We laughed about it because Pete's mom still wouldn't be able to get into his new car—the Corvette—with all her groceries, too.

✦

PATRICIA BLUM *recounts the Sunday football games in which Ed and Rose played:*

They played a lot of their home games at Cole Rain High School. It was a rowdy group of guys. There were some different age groups of guys playing in those games, with some of the guys a lot older than the rest. At that time, you wouldn't think of Pete Rose as anybody out of the ordinary. Like most guys, Pete would often have his girlfriend there watching the games.

It really was a rough team. I remember going to a banquet they had at the end of the season, and it turned into a free-for-all. One of the fellows on the team who already had suffered a broken leg got into a fight with one of the other players, and crutches were being swung and stuff like that. That's when I said to Ed, "Time to leave. Football season is over."

✦

PAT THOMAS, *one grateful underclassman befriended by Rose at Western Hills, recalls running into Pete many years later:*

Although I never knew him well, I knew him just enough that he still recognized me years later. I had a couple of nieces who were in the same graduating class as Pete's daughter (Fawn) at Oak Hills High School. I saw Pete at the same graduating ceremony, sitting about two or three rows behind us.

My son Brian, who was about eight at the time, saw Pete sitting back there, and whispered to me, "Dad, Dad, Dad— that's Pete Rose sitting back there! Pete Rose. Pete Rose!" Brian was going nuts, and I tried to tell him that this was a

graduation ceremony and that Pete didn't want to be bothered by anybody.

"Oh, c'mon, Dad. I gotta ask him; I gotta ask him." Brian
wanted to go back and get an autograph. Finally, I took out
a business card and gave it to him so he could go get Pete's
autograph. "Now don't you monkey with him," I said to my
son. "Be nice, because he's here trying to enjoy the ceremony
and probably doesn't want to be bothered." But my boy was
so eaten up with baseball, that I figured the worst thing that
could happen was for Pete to tell him to get the hell away.

My son went up there and gave the card to Pete for him
to sign. I don't know whether it was because he looked on
the card and recognized the name and saw me sitting there,
or what, but he went ahead and gave Brian a signature on
the back of the business card. Now that Pete makes a lot of
money selling his autograph, there's a lot of horror stories
going around about that. But every time I hear a horror story
about Pete and autographs and money, I tell them about my
son's experience and what a heckuva guy Pete was. Pete
showed a lot of class in that particular instance.

JOHN REWWER *offers this final observation of Pete
Rose, high school student-athlete:*

In high school he was pretty much a normal guy, maybe a bit
cocky. He wasn't big man on campus, yet everyone knew who
he was. He was nice to about everybody, but he wasn't someone you would consider the most popular guy in school.

One summer while I was working downtown, I was with
a buddy of mine and we ran into Pete on a street corner. I
asked him what was up, and he said he was downtown to
meet a girl for lunch, and then he pointed across the street,
saying, "And that's her right over there." It was Karolyn,
who would go on to become his wife.

There was this certain girl who Pete had always dated in high school. She was really well-endowed, the whole package, and she never got over him. I knew a girl who lived next door to this girlfriend of Pete's and asked her whatever happened to this girl, and my friend said, "She's just so messed up because of Pete." The last I heard she was living over in Covington with some old man.

2

◆

CHARLIE HUSTLE

P ete Rose detractors can always find ways to put asterisks next to his name.

All-time hits leader? Well, they say, he should be. He played in 527 more games than Ty Cobb did and had over 2,500 more at-bats, enough to make up for the fact that his career batting average was more than sixty points below that of the Georgia Peach's.

One of baseball's greatest players? Please. We're talking about a guy who never really found a home in the field, playing only 26.4 percent of his career games at his most-occupied spot—first base.

Great winner and champion, playing on six pennant winners and three World Series champions? Like he did it all by himself? Not. At Cincinnati, Rose had Johnny Bench,

Joe Morgan, Tony Perez, Dave Concepcion, and Sparky Anderson. With the Phils, he had Steve Carlton, Mike Schmidt, Greg Luzinski, Larry Bowa, and Bake McBride. Bob Uecker or "Marvelous" Marv Throneberry could have won a World Series ring with either of those teams.

One category that, indisputably, doesn't get an asterisk is hustle. No player in baseball history ran everything out the way Rose did. Running to first base on walks. Running out grounders all the way. Stretching singles into doubles. Chasing balls down in the gaps. Even the headfirst slides. Some of it was theatrical, perhaps even unnecessary. But it was great stuff, and it was great for the game. Where have you gone, Pete Rose?

Rose didn't just start going the extra mile when he got to the majors; he started almost as soon as he learned how to walk. He hustled in Knothole Baseball and all the way through high school. He hustled while playing high school football, and he kept on hustling throughout his baseball career. Opposing players, even some teammates, ridiculed him and mocked him for it, but when all was said and done, few could honestly say that they thought he was wrong.

Rose gave baseball fans a terrific show for almost twenty-five years, and he brought a lot of excitement into the game. He did this every day. Until the Big Red Machine unveiled itself in the early seventies, all Cincinnati really had to show from 1963 until Sparky Anderson's arrival in 1970 was a hotshot Rose, gunning for batting titles while banging out hits and running everything out.

Rose was paid very well in large part because of his Charlie Hustle shtick. No other major-league ballplayer has come close to attempting Rose's level of hustle. What are they waiting for? Permission from Donald Fehr? Hard-charging players of Rose's ilk would bring some pizzazz to a game badly in need of it, as Commissioner Bud Selig might agree. Then again, maybe the players union wouldn't go for it.

Are there any players' agents out there with the guts to tell their clients to put a little Pete Rose into their game— just a modicum of hustle to go with their juiced-up swagger? Baseball could use a fix that isn't chemical, even if comical at times.

Charlie Hustle, on the field, was a role model, an overachiever, a winner, a producer, and wonderful entertainment. That part of him was pretty special. Any takers?

RICHARD HAUCK, himself a Western Hills High School grad, was a reserve coach at Western Hills when Rose attended school there. He had a hand in coaching Pete, both in baseball and football. By the time Rose in 1960, and three years before he even joined the Reds, he had secured his reputation as a hustler, even though he didn't officially have the nickname yet. Hauck:

Sports was everything to Pete. Education wasn't that important. He did enough to get by.

He was a hustler, although I had his younger brother, Dave, a few years later, and I thought Dave was a better player while in high school than Pete had been. But Pete worked so hard. When he signed a pro contract (in 1960), Pete weighed 165 pounds. When he came back a couple of years later, he weighed 195, and you would see him always swinging a baseball bat. He made himself into a good ballplayer.

You've got to admire the guy. He didn't have a heckuva lot of talent, but what he did have he used and developed to the maximum.

He's likable. He would give you the shirt off your back. And he will always recognize you no matter where you are— he'll come up and pat you on the back and talk to you. But he has changed, and I wish he would shape up a little bit so that he could get into the Hall of Fame, because he belongs there. You'd think he would keep his nose clean, but I've seen where he's allegedly still gambling and running around.

⚬

*Like Hauck, **GLENN SAMPLE** first saw Rose as a young boy with a lot of ambition, and was amazed at how much Rose continued to grow and develop physically after he left high school. Then there was the ever-present hustle:*

For a while Pete dated a girl who lived near where my mother's house was, so I would see him quite a bit, and this was soon after he had signed with the Reds. By this time, you could see that he was starting to grow and fill out a bit. You could see that he was maturing.

I asked him how he was doing one time, and he said, "Oh, man, I'm swinging a weighted bat six hundred times a day, three hundred times left-handed and three hundred times right-handed. I'm going to work on my footwork, and they're getting ready to send me to the Instructional League, where I can learn about turning the double play. I am really looking forward to that."

You could tell from his attitude that all he really wanted to do was to play ball.

⚬

*Noted political essayist and baseball lover **GEORGE WILL** summed up his appreciation for Rose's work ethic in a 1991 column, a portion of which follows:*

Rose spent five years in high school in Cincinnati, repeating his sophomore year, which he had flunked. Then he went into professional baseball, weighing 155 pounds. He was carrying his father's heavy expectations and, (writer James) Reston says, wearing "the desperation of his situation on his sleeve." Remember the famous report on Fred Astaire's first screen test? "Can't act. Slightly bald. Can dance a little." The Reds' scouting report on the puny switch-hitting infielder said:

"Can't make a double play, can't throw, can't hit left-handed, and can't run." At that time the report was correct, but it missed an ingredient—Rose's fanatical concentration of his meager athletic gifts on whatever task was at hand.[1]

ED BRINKMAN, *who would go on to a long major-league career of his own that included long stints with the Washington Senators and Detroit Tigers, was the more attractive baseball prospect coming out of Western Hills, although Rose gradually would surpass his former teammate in the big leagues:*

Pete was a great teammate. Very enthusiastic. Played with a lot of energy. Always hustled, even back then, before he became known as Charlie Hustle. Actually, he had the ability, but no one noticed it yet because he was so small.

He always played hard. He had just started switch-hitting when I met up with him in high school, and each day he just kept getting a little better from the left side. Anytime you have a player that plays with that kind of hustle, that kind of intensity, its pretty impressive. People used to say to me, "Why don't you play like Pete?" Well, I was about six-foot and weighed about 150, and if I ran that hard all the time, when the season was over I would have weighed about 130 or 140 and I'd be exhausted. Pete didn't start growing up until after he signed.

Peter was a very, very hard worker. He wanted to be a big-league player, and that was in his head. He constantly was swinging the leaded bat. There were a couple of years there when he and I ran around together during the winters of our minor-league days. He would call me at seven in the morning and say, "Let's go!" I'd say, "Peter, it's only seven o'clock in the morning."

He'd say, "Let's go to the gym and play catch, or roll some groundballs to each other."

Pete was getting bigger and stronger every year, and it all came together for him.

⊏⬥⊐

TOMMY HELMS, *for many years a teammate of Rose in Cincinnati, and later a coach under Rose during the latter's stint as Reds manager, followed a career track similar to Pete's. They were an infield combination dating back to the minor leagues, with Helms at short and Pete at second. Rose would win the National League Rookie of the Year Award in 1963; Helms would do so in 1966. It's no wonder they became good friends. Helms:*

I met him in 1961, at spring training with the Reds. Here was a guy who hustled all the time—even in spring training. Nonstop. A lot of people were calling him a hotdog and all that stuff, and that's just the way he was. He ran everything out. He was a guy who stuck out just a little bit. He wasn't a gifted player, but he made himself into a good player.

We first played together in Macon (Georgia). We had a good team—a lot of us went to the big leagues, including our manager (Dave Bristol). Pete and I were a second baseman/shortstop combination—I hit .340 and he hit .330, and that's just unheard of for two middle infielders on the same team.

After the 1962 season, we got invited back to spring training. I had just hit .340, and back then they didn't give raises. I think they wanted to give me a twenty-five-dollar-a-month raise. I didn't think I could make it on $450 a month. People couldn't make any money in those days, but then Pete went and made the big club and made Rookie of the Year.

Scouts weren't banging on Pete's door when he was in high school. Only after one of his uncles, a part-time Reds bird-dog (an unpaid scout) named Buddy Bloebaum, pleaded with Reds brass to take a chance on the hometown boy, did they offer Rose a piece of paper with a dotted line. His signing bonus was five thousand dollars, less than a tenth what his high school teammate Ed Brinkman had gotten from the Senators. **JOHN REWWER,** *another of Rose's Western Hills schoolmates,* remembers Pete's reaction to the signing:

Soon after Pete bought that Corvette with his signing money from the Reds, he spun it out in front of my house one day.

REWWER *adds this:*

Pete loved the game, and he really worked at it. Tommy Helms said to me one time, "Back in Charlotte (North Carolina), there are a lot better baseball players than Pete is, but it's all a matter of timing and being able to perform at the right time."

Pete had this cockiness about him that once you put him in position to do something, he just took right off and they couldn't get him out, and he just kept working his way up to the majors.

He never drank or smoked, but he did chase the women.

First stop on Rose's rise to the majors was Geneva,
New York. Geneva resident CHARLES HICKEY's family
rented a room to Pete when he was playing there.
Hickey:

Rose was a great holler guy—not that everybody liked what
he hollered. He came out with some pretty good terms. You
know, it's a small ballpark. The fans sitting close could hear
the terms he used. Some of them would get upset.[2]

⊐◇⊏

EDDIE SMALDONE was a supporter of Geneva's minor-
league team:

Even in Geneva he was a hard-nosed ballplayer. He wasn't
too fancy a fielder, but if a ball was hit his way, he'd stop it
with his chest, pick it up, and throw the guy out. He got the
job done.

He was always running, hustling. I couldn't tell you a
whole lot about his personality, except that he was a cocky
little kid. He had a little trouble running off at the mouth
sometimes, but what the hell, a lot of guys did that.

You go back to Geneva now and you'll find at least ten
people who will all claim that they rented a room to Pete
while he was in town.

⊐◇⊏

SMALDONE, about Geneva:

There's actually two Genevas—the town of Geneva, where I
now live, and the city of Geneva. If you go forty miles to the
west, you are in Rochester, and fifty miles east takes you into
Syracuse. It's right in the heart of the Finger Lakes, which is
now coming into its own because of the beauty of the place.

At one time Geneva used to be a bustling center. It was

back in the forties when they built an ordnance depot, where they stored ammunition. Then in '41, they built a naval base, and that was a big, big undertaking. There was something like thirty-five or forty thousand recruits there at all times. Then they shut it down in 1946, after the war, and it became a college. It was reactivated in 1951 as an air force base, and that got to be a big deal.

Geneva was a boomtown in those eras, with people and businesses moving in.

By the time Pete got here, Geneva was no longer an air force or navy town. The baseball team was a pretty big deal, and they used to draw pretty well. But then, there wasn't too much else to do, except play softball, and softball was a big deal in these parts. Many kids couldn't afford a baseball glove in those days, so they played softball.

The caliber of baseball was pretty good, and there were some pretty good rivalries. Our ballpark sat about fifteen hundred, although they could jam two thousand in there when they wanted to. On average, we would get about eight hundred to a thousand for a game.

It was a small town, where everybody knew each other, and the players were real close to the fans at the ballpark. This wasn't Yankee Stadium, where you sit a mile away from the players on the field. They were close enough here to where they got to know the players.

In those days, it would take a stretch to see Pete Rose as a future great player in the majors. But take Tony Perez— that guy could really hit the ball. And then there was Art Shamsky, who was a heck of an outfielder.

DAVE BRISTOL, *who would join Rose on the Reds as manager during the 1965 season, first linked up with Rose in 1961 on Pete's second stop en route to the major leagues:*

I first saw Pete in spring training in 1961, and the first year he played for me was in 1962 in Macon, Georgia. He was just a baby, just getting started. The first thing I noticed about him was his energy. He had grown up to play baseball, and that's all he thought about. He was fun to be around and fun to manage.

When he first got to pro ball, there might have been some things about him that questioned his baseball ability, but there were some intangibles that you had to like about Pete Rose. Over time he got bigger, he got stronger, and he got faster. Part of the reason he got bigger and faster was by working for Coca-Cola over the winter, lifting those twenty-four-bottle cartons of Coke for hours on end.

He just loved to play so much that he had an inner drive that you seldom see in ballplayers.

-◁◇▷-

BRISTOL, *again:*

Pete was the greediest player I ever had . . . and that's no knock. A lot of players, when they get a couple of hits up front, they cruise. Particularly if the game is one-sided. They don't bear down on their last at-bats. Not Pete."[3]

-◁◇▷-

One of Rose's minor-league roommates was outfielder
MEL QUEEN JR., *who would eventually make it to the Reds in 1964 and later become a pitcher:*

We talked baseball constantly. We'd stay up until two or three in the morning talking baseball, and then we'd finally go to sleep.

Bright and early at eight o'clock, he'd be up and I'd be in a coma. He'd come over to me and shake me, yelling, "C'mon, Queenie, we're going to the park! We're going to the park!"

"Pete, it's eight o'clock in the morning. Leave me alone."

"No, c'mon. We're going to go and work on some things."

He was just driven. He got by on just four or five hours of sleep a night. I'd ask him, "Pete, are you on pills? Are you on speed? Are you on something?"

One year in the Instructional League, Tommy Helms and I roomed together with Pete. We'd play those games at, like, ten o'clock in the morning when it was already a hundred degrees, then afterward we would go back to the apartment, have a little nap, and then go out to dinner and have a few drinks. Pete did not drink, but Tommy and I drank.

We'd get back to the apartment at about eleven or twelve o'clock at night, and Tommy and I would have a pretty good buzz on. Then at seven o'clock in those days, Pete would wake us up, and Tommy and I would be throwing stuff at him to shut him up. "Leave us alone."

"No, we gotta go to the park, we gotta go to the park. We've got to get ready for the game, we've got to get ready for the game. We're gonna win the game today!" We're gonna do this; we're gonna do that. He was just driven.

If Pete had had the mind of Bill Gates, he would have left Gates in the dust simply because of his drive and determination. Never give up.

I once had a talk with Jack Fisher, a pitcher who pitched with, among other teams, the Reds and Mets. Jack had a great changeup, and he told me, "Before I die, I'm going to get Pete Rose out with my changeup." You see, Pete Rose couldn't hit a good fastball because he had a slow bat. But what he could do when you threw a good fastball was flare it off into left field.

Every time Fisher would try to throw a changeup past Pete, Pete would hit a bullet into right center. Finally, Fisher said, "Well, I've tried getting my changeup past him eighteen times, and eighteen times he's gotten a hit off of me. I've given up. He can hit my changeup."

⊏◇⊐

BRISTOL fondly remembers his days managing the likes of Rose and Helms in Macon:

There were some good ballplayers on that team, such as Tommy Helms who played alongside Pete and outhit him by about ten points. It was a fun ballclub, too, and very team-oriented. We finished second or third in the regular season and then won the playoffs without losing a game.

Macon was a heckuva good place, a good Southern town that you can't say anything bad about—I was born there. It was a good town, and we had an excellent sportswriter who really liked baseball and gave us a lot of good coverage, and the Reds put some good players in there.

The Sally League (South Atlantic League) at the time was an excellent league. Knoxville, for example, at that time had guys like Jim Northrup, Willie Horton, Ray Oyler, and Mickey Stanley (who would later play on a World Series winner with the Detroit Tigers in 1968). Savannah had a good team, too, including Dave DeBusschere, who would later play pro basketball.

We traveled in three station wagons, with a U-Haul behind one of them for carrying all of the equipment. Players were always jockeying for position in the cars and their turn to drive. Now that I think about it, I can't remember ever ending up in the same car with Pete. I don't think he was try-ing to stay away from me; it just worked out that way.

Most teams had buses, and with the players driving the station wagons, you just lived on pins and needles hoping that nothing bad would happen to them on the roads. On one trip, we were headed from Portsmouth, Virginia, to Savannah, Georgia, when one of the cars got a flat tire at about three or four o'clock in the morning. We got in late that day, and then we had to go play that night.

There weren't any short road trips—it was a haul everywhere we went. Yeah, it was a lot of miles, but when you are around a bunch of young guys like that, you don't worry about the distances so much.

PHOTO COURTESY OF CINCINNATI REDS

BRISTOL *saw Rose as a definite clubhouse asset:*

A young, switch-hitting Pete Rose bats from the left side as a brash new Reds player.

Pete liked to kid around a lot. We had a good rapport in the clubhouse all the time, and he was part of it. He kept the banter going all the time, and as far as I could tell, he was well liked.

He really cared about himself. He cared about the way he looked. He cared about the way he dressed.

TOMMY HELMS:

At Macon, we would usually pay a guy fifty bucks a month extra to drive. We had a big U-Haul on the back of one of the cars. We got pretty good at hitting those road signs with Coke bottles out the window. It wasn't how good an arm you had but a matter of timing.

Back then we went all the way up to Lynchburg, Virginia, and there were a lot of long rides in there. What I remember about playing in the Sally League was how hot it was almost every place we went. Going to Asheville up in North Carolina was like going to San Francisco, by comparison. It was cool up there in the mountains of North Carolina.

⌖

*Pitcher MEL QUEEN was one of many Reds who
bumped into Rose on their way up to the majors:*

The only reason Pete was signed in the first place was that he was from Cincinnati. Back then, the scouting reports categorized guys as D, C, B, A, Double-A, and Triple-A. If Pete had been from Dayton or Lima, Ohio, he probably never would have been signed. The report on Pete said that he would be a Class-C filler. That meant, at best, they thought he could be a utility ballplayer for a Class-C ball club. But sometimes you do someone a favor for a guy, and it turns out great.

If you broke down his tools, maybe his running speed and arm could pass muster. Everything else was below average. His swing was one of the ugliest swings I have ever seen. There were so many players in the Cincinnati organization that had so much more natural ability than Pete Rose, but none of them had Pete Rose's heart or desire.

I remember playing with him in Macon and taking one look at that swing and saying, "Oh my God!" He had stiff hands playing second base. He also had great confidence in himself, and he just felt he was going to be a superstar. And he would let nothing or nobody step in his way.

I roomed with him for a while, and I think he had more energy than anyone else has ever had playing a particular sport. Maybe Walter Payton had the same thing, and maybe Michael Jordan, for their sports. Pete had this for baseball. He lived and died baseball.

⌖

*In 1962, Rose played for the minor-league club in
Tampa, Florida, his last stop in the minors before going*

to the big time a year later. **JOHNNY "DOUBLE NO-HIT" VANDER MEER,** *Rose's manager at Tampa,:*

We had a lot of young players we were looking at for the Tampa, club. We had a pretty good idea of who our starting players would be, or we thought we had a pretty good idea. Pete was on the scrubinis, the second team. . . . The scrubinis were all the kids who didn't know nothing. We played them against the regulars to evaluate whether we were gonna keep them or release them. Pete would run and dive and slide headfirst. I'm not patting myself on the back, but I made a pretty darn good evaluation. I told the Reds I wanted to keep this kid. He was going to be something.[4]

Adds **VANDER MEER:**

He got off to a real good start. Every time I looked up, he was driving one into the alleys and running like a scalded dog and sliding headfirst into third. He hit thirty triples for me that year. Led the league. . . .He just hit the ball real well from both sides of the plate. He was hitting .350 up until midseason, when the average started to drop but not very much. (Rose batted .331 in 1961.)

When you get a young player hitting .350 for you, you let him alone. I'm a firm believer in not overcoaching. The only thing I ever told Pete was, "Make sure you get a good ball to hit. Don't swing at the bad ones."[5]

The story goes that Rose got his "Charlie Hustle" nickname during spring training one year when he ran out a walk in an exhibition game against the Yankees, and Whitey Ford yelled from the New York dugout, "Hey, look at Charlie Hustle!" **ROSE:**

I wouldn't say I mind it. I've sure gotten good mileage out of it, if you count up all those columns of ink. But it isn't exactly right. I want to get what I'm saying now precise. *Hustle* may be just a little downgrading, like I don't have a lot of skills, you know? I do have outstanding skills—who's had better hand-to-eye coordination?—and I got the most out of them, sure, but not so much with hustle as with enthusiasm. All these years, from the first pro game in Geneva, New York, in 1960 until today, I haven't lost one damn bit of enthusiasm for baseball. That's why I've been able to work so hard. So maybe we need a new nickname. What do you say? "Eddie Enthusiasm?" Probably never catch on like Charlie Hustle.[6]

As a rookie in 1963, Rose was unpopular with a number of Reds veterans who were pals of incumbent second baseman Don Blasingame, an eight-year veteran who had batted a very respectable .281 the year before. JAMES RESTON JR., *author of* Collision at Home Plate*:*

Predictably, the veterans began to turn on Pete. They made fun of his grandstanding, made cracks about his alpaca sweaters and his language and the gap in his teeth, and snubbed him overtly. . . . So Rose turned to Frank Robinson and Vada Pinson, the two best players on the team, who themselves formed a daunting and troublesome clique. The black superstars welcomed him, for they knew all about snubs. This was 1963, and in Florida and elsewhere in the South, Robinson, despite his .342 average and Most Valuable Player Award in 1961, and Pinson, with his .343 average in 1961, often had to eat in the bus or in their rooms. . . .

One night Rose's teammate bolted the door at midnight. (In the player's defense, he seemed to have a late-night visitor.) Rose wandered down to Pinson's room, where he was greeted warmly and given a bed. In the morning Pinson ordered his customary room-service breakfast—an extravagance to Rose but a necessity to Pinson—and a lasting friendship was forged. From Robinson and Pinson, Rose learned other social amenities, such as how to tip and how to dress. "Nobody had to show Pete how to hit," Robinson was to say years later, "but they wouldn't even show him how to be a major-leaguer. So we did."[7]

VADA PINSON, *on Rose as a rookie:*

We were upset, too. We couldn't understand why Blasingame was being edged out. But Frank and I had been through plenty of discrimination ourselves—having to board with black families in spring training because we couldn't stay in the team hotel, being barred from certain restaurants. The way Pete was being treated was not something we were going to go for.

It upset me. He was a rookie, untried. But he had a uniform on, he was a teammate, and we were trying to win. The way I was raised was to treat people as human beings, fellow human beings. I think that's all we did with Pete.[8]

This from **FRANK ROBINSON,** *excerpted from his book* **Extra Innings:**

No other players warmed to Rose all season, so Vada and I became his friends and showed him the ropes around the league. We'd warm up together throwing a ball around before games. After games, if Vada and I were going out for a bite to eat, we always tried to bring Pete along. He loved to talk baseball as much as I did. Being black and having gone through some hard times with aloneness myself, I felt for Pete, and he said he appreciated my thinking of him.[9]

✦

MEL QUEEN *knew Rose some from the minors, and they would be teammates for four seasons in Cincinnati, from 1966 through 1969. Queen:*

Pete Rose was not ready for the big leagues when they took him up, but he was from Cincinnati. If anybody should have been given a shot in the big leagues in 1963, it should have been Tommy Helms. He batted something like .350 that year, and ended up leading the Sally League in doubles when he hit something like four doubles in our last game.

Pete got the shot, and he did the job. It just goes to show, you've got to be real careful when talking about a player, saying he's got no chance. Pete goes up that first year, and against a lot of expectations, batted .273 and won the National League's Rookie of the Year Award. So baseball experts don't always know.

I played with a lot of great players, but the only one I've ever known who comes close to Pete in terms of having confidence in himself was Frank Robinson. He may have been a better team player than Pete Rose, because what Frank would do is go to the young kids and say, "Hey, you did this, but this is what you need to do," and he would make the younger guys into better players. He schooled the young players.

One time we were playing in Houston, and Don Wilson was due to pitch, and he was nasty. But Wilson came up hurt, and so the Astros brought up some lefthander from the minors to pitch against us. In the clubhouse before the game, Frank was saying, "I don't like this. I don't know this guy. Don Wilson—I know how he'll pitch to me. This other guy, I don't know what he's going to do."

Pete on the other hand said, "Hey, I don't care. This guy still has to throw the ball over the plate to do anything, and when he does, I'll hit it." In those respects, Frank and Pete were both confident players, but there was a little bit of a difference there.

When Rose got to the Reds in 1963, he joined a team of mostly veterans that just two years earlier had gone to the World Series. One of those veterans was pitcher JIM O'TOOLE, *who recalls those early days of 1963 with a certain cocky newcomer:*

Pete was a brash young rookie in 1963. Don Blasingame had hit .281 the year before and was a well-liked guy on the team. And he was a good second baseman on top of all that.

Pete came to spring training and hustled, and somehow Hutch (Reds manager Fred Hutchinson) took a liking to the way he played the game. Plus there was the fact that while Blasingame was looking to make twenty to twenty-five thousand dollars, Pete was only making five thousand, which was a big difference back then. Still, I was really surprised when Hutch picked Pete ahead of Blasingame to be the starting second baseman.

Pete did some things that year that most rookies wouldn't even attempt to do. We had this one spring-training trip to Mexico City, where he pretty much displayed the type of brashness that he had. I wasn't there because I didn't have to make the trip, but a couple of guys on the team told me the story, and there were several writers there.

They went to some joint down there, and they had some stripper come over to their table. Evidently Pete called over to the table and, bingo, he had her down on the table doing something no one should be doing in public.

Everybody knew about it, but no one did anything about it. I broke in a few years earlier than that, and if I had done something like that as a rookie, I would have found myself right back down in Double-A. But Pete got away with a lot of stuff that normal players couldn't have gotten away with. He was just different.

Part of the deal was that it's unusual to have a local kid make the team, and I guess the Reds were determined to stick with him because when he got between the white lines, he could really make things happen. Blasingame couldn't believe what was happening; he never got an opportunity. He didn't get much playing time in spring training, and before you knew it he was gone.

*Rose's growing clubhouse friendship with Frank Robinson and Vada Pinson caught the eye of a number of veterans, **O'TOOLE** included:*

You've got to remember, this was still the early sixties, and I had never seen it happen before, where a white man would be sitting on the floor in front of a black player sitting on his seat in front of him, and he'd be shining their shoes while talking to them in that black jabber. Like, "What it is, man," and "Where we goin' tonight, man?" I couldn't believe it—not that he would talk to black players but that he would practically grovel toward them.

*The fact that Robinson and Pinson were willing to take Rose under their wing is a credit to them, but there still were other things that Rose did that raised a lot of eyebrows and further kept him at arm's length from many teammates. **O'TOOLE**:*

One of the things you learn early on as a ballplayer is that you don't take your wife with you when you're going out after a game with the guys. Then there's Pete. He would take Karolyn out with him to places where there might be a married teammate or two talking to a couple of stewardesses at the bar. Then Karolyn might walk up to these other guys, put her arm around them, and say, "Hey, don't worry about it. Have a good time. I won't tell your wives. I know Pete does stuff when he's on the road, but as long as he doesn't mess around while he's home, I don't give a crap."

All Pete was thinking about was having a good time, although one thing he didn't do was drink. Here's a rookie with a wife who has his same mentality. Peter finally got to the point where he would bring other women right in front of his wife's face, and they would be wearing the same jewelry that he had given to her and would be sitting right behind home plate. It was crazy.

KAROLYN ROSE, *née Karolyn Englehardt, likewise was a Cincinnati native with an outgoing personality of her own. She recalls how she met Pete and fell in love:*

I met Pete in July 1963, and we got married six months later. He had a good personality, even though I hadn't known who he was.

I met him at the racetrack, Riverdale. He was with a guy who I knew, and I was with some other fellow at the racetrack. They introduced us to each other. That's when I said to Pete, "Don't you play football for some local team?" I really didn't know who he was, that he was a player for the Cincinnati Reds.

A few days later, while I was at work, working for American Book Company, I'm told that there is a phone call for me, some guy named Pete. I get to the phone, answer it, and this guy says, "Karolyn?" I said, "Yessss."

"This is Pete."

"Pete who? I know a couple of Petes."

He said, "Pete Rose. Would you like to go to the game tonight?"

"Oh, no, no. I have a date with somebody else for tonight."

Well, he kept calling and calling. Finally, I said okay, but he would first have to meet my family. That was a prerequisite in our Catholic family. My mother had always told me, "Show me your company, and I'll tell you who you are."

So Pete came over to our house and met my family. He had another game that night, and he said, "Why don't we drive over to the ballpark? You can drop me off and then come back here and get dressed for the game, then be back at the ballpark in time for the start of the game."

Now that was pretty neat. Here's a guy already willing to let me use his car, a Grand Prix. Classy guy. I went down to the ballpark, got my ticket, and sat down in front. After the game, I waited for him, and he took me out to eat at the Busy Bee, a restaurant down in Clifton.

What was funny was that I was smoking at the time, and he asked me if he could have one of my cigarettes. I said, "Sure." So he lit one of them up and started choking on the smoke, as if he was about to die. He said, "Man, these are really strong." And I said, "Pete, do you even smoke?" He had never smoked in his life. He was just trying to impress me.

I was twenty-one, and he was twenty-two.

KAROLYN ROSE, *on their early years together as husband and wife:*

In the early going, Pete wasn't making much money. So after we got married in January, we lived with my parents in their house for three years. That was fun. Pete got to eat well there.

We lived on the third floor of the house. It was a three-family house, and my dad finished out the third floor by putting in a full bath, bedroom, living room, and kitchen. But we never cooked up there because there was no stove. My mother always cooked, and that was great because then we could go downstairs and eat together, and then go back up to our third-floor living area.

We had Fawn on December 29, 1964. That fall, following the season, I had accompanied Pete to Venezuela where he was going to play winter ball. Our plan was to have the baby while down there. After we got down there, though, one of the other players broke his hand. I think it was Bill Freehan, the catcher. The day after he went to the emergency room to get his hand taken care of, he told me that he had seen what he thought was a rat run across the floor of the emergency room. At that point, I decided I was going to go back home to Cincinnati to have the baby. I left in late October.

That was the first and last time Pete played winter ball.

⋘⚬⋙

PETE ROSE once had this to say about what it was like for him, being a rookie with the Reds:

When I was a kid and my dad couldn't get to Crosley Field, I'd hang around outside. Skinny little crew-cut kid, and I'd go up to strangers and say, "Got an extra ticket, mister?" Sometimes it worked. Sometimes I got into the ballpark that way. And now the guys I'd begged my way in to see—Spahn, Stan Musial—like that, I was playing major-league ball on the same field with them. And in the town where I grew up. I was still skinny and crew-cut when I was twenty-two.[10]

⋘⚬⋙

Rose, *appraising his defensive skills:*

I knew myself as an outfielder. I'd never say I had the arm of a (Roberto) Clemente or a Carl Furillo, because I never did. But my years in the infield made me a better outfielder. It's all one game. At second I had to learn to charge the ball hard. I took that with me into the outfield. I got to the ball quick, and I got rid of it quick. Take a slower man than me, or someone who can't charge balls like I could, it pretty much balances out arm strength.

I know a great throw is spectacular, but I think that's one part of baseball that gets overrated, just because it is so spectacular. You know how many major-league games I played? Three thousand five hundred and sixty-two. The most ever. The most anybody ever played. How many of those ended with a guy being thrown out at the plate? I don't have a stat for that, but very, very few.[11]

⊏✧⊐

Jim O'Toole *offers this assessment of Rose:*

In the eight years that I played with the Reds, he was probably the worst second baseman we ever had. He could not make the double play. He had real slow hands and no arm at all. When he ran, it looked like he was running fast, but he really wasn't going that fast. But the one thing he could do was hit the cover off the ball.

There were some guys on the team—we had our cliques in those days, too—who would go around telling guys they knew on the opposite team that the way to pitch Pete was with smoke, blow him away. Still, Pete would end up hitting line drives all over the place, even against these pitchers that had been tipped off by our own guys.

⊏✧⊐

Between 1963 and 1969, the Reds were somewhat of an enigma. Offensively, they packed a pretty good punch, and they had flashes of brilliant pitching, led by one of the most underrated great flamethrowers of the time, Jim Maloney. Yet, the Reds didn't win a pennant in Rose's first seven years with the club. They finished third once (1964) and fourth twice (1967 and 1968) when league play was a ten-team battle, and third again (in 1969) in the National League West. The Reds were consistently good, but never great. MEL QUEEN remembers, focusing on a 1964 stretch run in which the Reds won nine straight late in the season to forge a one-game lead with five games left. Following a 2–0 loss to the Pirates, the Reds had a chance to redeem themselves, needing a win to regain a tie for first place:

Jim Maloney hooked up with the Pirates that night (against Bob Veale). It ended up going about sixteen innings. Five times after the ninth inning we had runners at first and third with one out, and we could never score a run. They ended up beating us on a squeeze play, 1–0. Still, we had a chance if we could beat the Phillies twice in a season-ending series.

Chris Short was pitching for the Phillies in the first game, and I knew they were down in the dumps because they'd had about a seven-game lead with ten games left to go and they'd blown it. We had maybe a two-run lead, with a guy on first and Leo Cardenas at bat, getting ready to bunt the guy over so we could further build onto our lead.

Short comes in with a high slider that just nicks Leo in the sleeve, but Leo charges the mound. So now we've got a fight. We break the fight up.

Dick Sisler was managing us at the point, having taken over after Fred Hutchinson passed away during the season. Dick chews Leo out for charging the mound, and the fight wakes up Philadelphia. As a result, Leo is really feeling down.

Jim O'Toole, "Tootie," was pitching for us. We go into the ninth inning still with a two-run lead. There's one out with a man on first, and pinch hitter Frank Thomas—playing with a cast on one hand because he's got a broken thumb—hits a little pop-up just to the left of the shortstop. Leo just stands there, and Pete comes all the way over from second and dives for it but just misses the ball. They go on to score three runs and beat us.

After the game, I knew some stuff was going to happen. I'm in the training room with Tootie, and he's fuming. Now here comes Leo. O'Toole charges Leo, and I grab Tootie. Then Leo runs out into the clubhouse to grab one of those spikes that the grounds crew uses. He's coming back into the training room, and when the rest of the players see that, they charge Leo.

About this time, Frank (Robinson) comes along, and all he sees is this bunch of guys charging Leo, not knowing what has transpired in the last few minutes. Frank goes to defend Leo, so the players turn on him. It turned out to be just a big rigmarole.

Then the next day—we still have a chance if we win and Saint Louis loses—we go to the park, and Maloney is set to pitch. He comes up with a ribcage injury, and the only guy we have left is John Tsitouris, a great guy. He comes to the park with his car all packed up, ready to head out to North Carolina after the game. He gets there and finds out point blank that he's going to start.

Now don't get me wrong, even though his car was packed, John goes out there and gives it his best. (Jim) Bunning pitches against us, and he beats us, 10–0. The Cardinals win, and they win the pennant.

At the time I didn't really know what it meant, but I look back now knowing that's the closest I ever came to playing in a World Series, and that was my rookie year.

⚏

Even though we didn't win a pennant in Pete's first seven years with the Reds, I never saw him get frustrated, even considering how much he wanted to win.

Pete was a guy who said, "I have a job to do. I'm going to do my job. Now, Queenie, you have a job to do. Tony Perez, so do you. Johnny Bench, you have a job to do. Tommy Helms, you have a job to do."

Pete felt each individual had a job to do, and, unfortunately, not many people could do the job the way Pete did it. He put so much confidence into other players, that he could bring a lesser player up to a higher caliber of playing ability. Without Pete there, there might not have been anyone else there to pick up that slack. A young guy looking at him running out ground balls and walks and hustling all over the field would look at this and have to say, "How can I do anything less than that?"

You can have twenty-five players putting out 100 percent and still not have things work out. Maybe you don't make the playoffs or the World Series. That's gonna happen. How many of the years that Henry Aaron played did the Braves not go to the postseason? Yet he was a guy who always worked his butt off?

At Cincinnati, Pete had the Big Red Machine and a group of great players that he helped make even better, and then he went to the Phillies and raised those players up a notch or two. Before Pete got to Philadelphia, Mike Schmidt was already a tremendous player, but maybe he needed someone to put a little tiny rocket in his backside, and Pete would be the one to do that. Pete would also be the guy who might come up to you after the game and say, "You know what? You didn't bear down in that situation. You've got to bear down." In that regard, I believe Frank Robinson was a big influence on Pete Rose.

What's happening in baseball today is that you don't have individuals like that, who will bear down all the time and help light a fire under other guys who aren't doing the same. It's unfortunate.

I remember one time when we were getting ready to play a game and I was in the outfield during batting practice. While the two teams were exchanging places in the field at one point, I ran into a guy, a friend of mine from California, and we stood there and talked for a long time. Later, Frank (Robinson) calls me over and says, "You know that guy?" I said, "Yeah, he's so-and-so from California."

"What's the name across his uniform?"

I said "Giants," although I'm not sure that's who we were playing. I don't remember.

He goes, "What's across your uniform?"

"Cincinnati."

"Then screw him. You want to go out to dinner with him after the game and all that, that's fine. But you don't talk to the opposition on the field. They're your enemy."

Years later, I was with the Angels and Frank was with Baltimore. They were taking infield practice, and Frank, naturally, was out in right field. I was down the right-field line because we were getting ready to take the field for outfield practice. When they came off the field, Frank jogged by me and without even looking at me or stopping his trot said, "Hey, Queenie, how ya doin'"? And without looking away from the outfield, I said, "Real good, Frank. How about you?" And that was it, and that's the way Frank was.

Frank had some input with Pete on how to be a pro competitor. Like the fight Pete had with Bud Harrelson. You know, Pete did nothing wrong on that play. He didn't throw a roll block or go in with his spikes up high. He just slid, put his foot out to hook the guy, and flipped him. That's the way Frank taught him.

Maury Wills once told me that the guy he feared most when on first base in case of a double-play ball was Frank Robinson. Frank taught me how to break up double plays, and I learned how just to kill infielders. And you don't get up and then help them up and pat them on the butt.

━❑━

JIM O'TOOLE was impressed by how Rose would sacrifice himself for the good of the team:

They moved Pete around, from second to third to the out-field and, finally, to first. That was the best spot for him because he had pretty good hands for handling a ball hit at him, and he didn't have to throw much.

Pete would always make that sacrifice for the good of the team. People will always remember him for his willingness to make room for George Foster in left field by moving to third base. And they ended up winning the World Series in '75 and '76 with the best ballclubs they ever had.

When it came to being a team leader, Pete wasn't a speechmaker or anything like that. What he did do was go out there every day and bust his butt out on the field. He led by his actions. I never saw him criticize players or anything of that nature. He just went out there and did his thing, as if to say, "Just watch me, man."

━❑━

Not all was well on the home front, as O'TOOLE explains:

There were a number of little things Pete did that, when added up, made a lot of guys not like him. He needed people around him to show him how better to conduct himself. One year they brought Johnny Temple over to try and help Pete, because he was a fiery guy just like Pete. Johnny was a better fielding second baseman, so they had him working with Pete in the field and also away from the field after the game. But it didn't work out, because finally it got to where Johnny would be looking for Pete after the game and Pete would be gone.

-⊶⊷-

JACK BALDSCHUN *spent two of his ten years in the majors with the Reds, in 1966 and 1967:*

I would put Pete in the same class as Lou Brock. They were both hustlers. Neither could hit the ball out of the infield when they first started. They were bad ballplayers, actually, but because they hustled and would even bunt to get on, they were kept around. Then both made themselves into good ballplayers by keeping at it. They started hitting line drives, and then a little power came with it later.

When you played against Pete, he was a real turkey. I could say worse words, but I won't. I remember hearing the Gene Mauch quote: "Let's stick one in his ear, then see how fast he goes to first on a walk." As a teammate of his, you had to like him because of his hustle.

As a person, he was totally different. He did everything his own way. He was Pete Rose, that's all. There were times that he thought everyone should look up to him, and that everything he did was right. You had good thoughts of him when you were playing with him and bad thoughts of him when you were playing against him.

It wasn't just that he would run to first base on a walk—-when he got there, he might stick out his tongue at you or just start yakking at you—all kinds of crap. He wasn't mature at all, and I still don't think he's mature. He's still waiting to grow up.

When he was playing for you, he went all out. He would do everything. As far as being a ballplayer with particular skills, he wasn't that good. He had bad hands and couldn't catch a ball. When he played third base, my God, all he could do was get in front of the ball, let it hit him in the chest, then pounce on it and, maybe, throw the guy out. He didn't have a good arm at all, which is why they played him at second base mainly.

I'll say this about him, though: I've never seen another guy who couldn't field, couldn't throw, and couldn't hit make himself into a good player like he did.

-◻-

TOMMY HELMS says one of Rose's strengths was his ability to put carrots out in front of himself, to set lofty goals and then go all out to achieve them:

Pete was good about setting new goals every year. One time he said he was going to be the first $100,000 singles hitter, and that happened. In other years, his benchmarks were two hundred hits, a hundred runs. Look at how many times that happened.

But the biggest thing to him was games played. I'll bet he played between 158 and 162 games a year for his first full ten seasons. That's incredible over that long a period. He didn't want a day off. He'd say, "I'll rest in November, December." He didn't want those four or five at-bats taken away from him, because the way he always figured it, he would get two hits out of that.

He watched his stats a lot, but he also led by example, as if to say, "Watch what I do." That was especially effective when he got a little older and more young guys started coming up. In watching Pete, they had to say, "Man, he's out there busting his butt every day. What am I going to do?"

People said that Pete might have been selfish in trying to reach his personal goals related to hits and stuff, but look

at it this way: the more hits he got, the more he was helping the team.

━◯━

**Things started turning around for the Reds once BOB
HOWSAM arrived on the scene as general manager:**

If I recall it right, they had Rose playing in the outfield by
the time I get there in 1967. He was playing left field. But he
was still a young ballplayer who, while a good player, could-
n't do some things in the field that maybe he could do better later on. Pete really became quite a fine asset to the Big
Red Machine when he got to third base.

━◯━

HOWSAM goes into more detail on Rose:

Pete Rose is extremely smart streetwise. I hadn't heard much
about Pete before I got to the Reds. I knew that he played
hard. The thing that impressed me the most about him was
his work ethic. He was a very hard worker, and he became a
great hitter because of that.

　　Rose is the greatest con artist I've ever seen on a baseball
field, and I say that in a positive way. He's not a speed
demon, couldn't throw very well, and had, at best, fair
hands. But he made you think all the time, and had a knack
for being able to make you think he might be doing things
he wasn't.

　　For instance, when I first got to the Reds, he was playing left field. I noticed how his hat kept coming off whenever he was chasing down a ball. So I went out there one day
to sit in the outfield stands to get a closer look at what was
going on. I remember wondering, *Can't the Reds find a hat for
this guy that fits?* But I was to find out that Pete was smart
enough to know that if people saw your hat coming off, they

would think that you are running fast and running from under that hat.

Same thing when he was running out a ball to first base, with his helmet flying off halfway down the baseline—they thought he was really tearing down there. Then after reaching first base, he would keep moving around and faking like he was going to go. Pitchers

PHOTO COURTESY OF CINCINNATI REDS

Even when he wasn't diving into base, Rose often would at least lose his helmet charging around the bases.

would keep throwing over there to hold him close. But if you look closely at any old films, you will see that he was never more than a step or two away from the bag.

If I were a pitcher in that situation, I would have figured it out sooner or later—*don't waste your time throwing over there.* It's when he took four steps off the bag that you knew Pete was going to go. But he made you think that he was going to steal a base. Go back and look at the statistics, and you will see that in 1975 he didn't steal a single base.

When he got a single, he would keep charging around first base, making the big turn. He was always thinking about the possibility of turning a single into a double, and many times he did just that.

*When it comes to hustling, pitcher **DICKIE NOLES**, a Phillies teammate of Rose for three seasons, says there are a couple of players over the past decade who compare favorably to Rose:*

Somewhere along the line, Sammy Sosa must have seen Pete Rose and something kicked in. When you see Sosa take the field, he takes it with some enthusiasm.

One guy who sticks out in my mind as being real similar to Pete in how hard he played—and he did it in a real quiet way—was Andre Dawson. He had a lot of the same baseball qualities that Pete did, but he wasn't as vociferous about it.

Pete's the type of guy who can act it, who can talk, who can rap—things like that. Andre's extremely quiet, but the way he did it was by hustling, example, and showing up every day. He's the guy that I've seen that comes closest to Pete in terms of playing hard every day. While Andre didn't run down to first base on walks, everything else he did, he did it in the same hustling manner. Awesome Dawson.

*Former pitcher **BILL "SPACEMAN" LEE** never played on a major-league team with Pete Rose, but he played against him on occasion, such as in the memorable 1975 World Series in which the Reds beat Lee's Boston Red Sox in seven games. Lee, on Charlie Hustle:*

The fact that he sprinted to first on a walk, an error, a single, and everything else bears it out. Pete was the epitome of what (former University of Southern California) baseball coach Rod Dedeaux said was the perfect lead-off hitter. Every time he hit the ball, he ran hard and was always thinking double or triple. That made outfielders work really hard to get the ball back into the infield, playing to hold him to a single. That aggressiveness puts pressure on your infield, your outfield, and your pitchers, putting everyone on edge.

When the (Montreal) Expos had their good years (in the early eighties), they had guys at the top of the batting order like Ron LeFlore, Tim Raines, Rodney Scott, and Andre Dawson—all guys who could put the ball into play and run the bases real aggressively. Good wheels are very influential in the game.

The reason we've never seen another player since Rose hustle the way he did, with the running to first on walks and the frequent headfirst slides, is because it's like it is with hunting dogs: When one dog is out front, no one gets past him because you've got to honor the big dog's point. There is a psychological mystique with that.

It's also like what has killed the National Basketball Association. It was Michael Jordan. He was so good, it has been hard to keep up with that. It's become a one-man game, with most teams having one hotshot who tries to be like Mike while the other four guys play a supporting cast. I miss the days when you had really good teams that could pass the ball around and had some truly good outside shooters with the big guy in the middle. Most of the guys you see now are a bunch of bricklayers—they can't shoot.

Pitcher **GEORGE CULVER** *played two seasons alongside Rose with the Reds and eight other years against him:*

I don't think anyone in the history of baseball has milked more out of his body to achieve what Pete did. Here's a guy playing 162 games a year, and it always looked like he was tickled to death just to be out there. The enthusiasm was always there. He had incredible energy, and he gave it his all on every play.

Pete couldn't run, but Pete did have some power, even if most people didn't realize it. I've seen it where he hit a home run from the left side in a game, and then turned around and hit one off the top of the fence right-handed. But he was smart enough to know that trying for home runs wasn't going to be his ticket to success.

One amazing thing about Pete was how he played a lot of positions. He didn't play any one of them particularly well, but I think he made the National League All-Star team at five different positions. I also read somewhere how he averaged fifty hits a month in September for many years. When most guys are tiring out late in the season, just trying to hang on and ready to go home, Pete was still going full speed and doing some of his best hitting.

*Rose really wasn't a superman, but he was an ironman. Take it from **LARRY STARR**, who as the Reds' trainer knew Rose well:*

One of the things he hated was for me to come out on the field. I think I went out after him twice in all the years he was with us. One time was on a pop-up down the left-field line. (Shortstop Dave) Concepcion pulled up short, and Pete went *pop*, right into the wall. He stayed in, but later his right elbow was all swollen and black and blue, and it had some fracture symptoms. I said after the game, "Let's get an x-ray," and he said, "No, I don't think so." And so we didn't. He just wouldn't do it.

Pete had this absolute confidence in his body. He didn't talk about it or think about it, that I know of. He wasn't a big off-season conditioner. He just figured it was gong to work and do the things he wanted it to do. And it did.[12]

GEORGE CULVER:

If every player did what Pete did, just from a hustle stand-point, the game would be really fun to watch. He averaged about forty doubles a year, and I guarantee you that at least half of those were really singles that he managed to stretch an extra base. He had a knack, from studying all the habits of outfielders in the league, of knowing whom he could run on. Pete didn't have great talent, but no one in the game has ever had a better work ethic.

With that work ethic came a sense of independence, as CULVER points out:

Pete had a certain amount of selfishness to him, but then baseball is a selfish game because so much of what is going on at any one time involves individual players. Pete always was very concerned with how he did in a game, whether he went 0–for–3 or 3–for–4 in a game and how each day's performance affected his stats.

There were times that he would really get on a roll and really suck it up, amassing hits like you wouldn't believe. And at any time during the season, if you stopped him and asked, he could run back through every one of his hits for the season and tell you whom he got the hit off of, what the situation was, and what the pitch was. It was awesome. He nailed it every time.

He also knew what was coming up. He could look ahead to whom our opponents would be for the next three series and run through their pitching rotations, knowing who he would be facing on any given day. Then after each game, he would go home and listen to a West Coast game, then come back to the ballpark the next day and tell you all about that game. And this was before the afternoon papers had come out, so you knew he was catching all this stuff on his own.

It was neat to be around a guy so driven like that, and yet he never abused his body with stuff like alcohol or cigarettes.

-=◇=-

CULVER *continues:*

Speaking of Pete's selfishness, I can remember a meeting we had in 1968, not long after I had gotten to the team. I didn't know many of the guys there, but I would soon get to know Pete a lot better, and real quickly.

During the team meeting, we were told that Marathon Oil had agreed to a promotion in which they would contribute fifty-five gallons of gas for every home run hit. Milt Pappas was our player rep running the meeting, during which Tony Perez stood up and asked, "What about the pitchers? What do they get?" He suggested that we put all the gas into a pool, so to speak, and divide it evenly among all the players.

Pete said, "No, I ain't doing that." Pete wanted to keep all the gas he earned for himself. Finally, (Johnny) Bench stood up and said, "Tell you what. I'll keep all the gas I get for the first fifteen home runs I hit, then after that, I'll split the rest." But not Pete—he was keeping all his for himself. Considering that Pete was hitting only five or six homers a year, he probably would have been better off agreeing to a team-wide split of the gas.

It was the same thing with doing a postgame radio show, in which players received Green Stamps for showing up and doing it. Pete wouldn't pass his around. He was a selfish teammate when it came to things like that.

There's only a handful of guys in baseball who would have done what Pete did when it came to the gas promotion. He was totally engrossed in himself, although I don't mean for that to sound negative. *Greedy* is probably a better word in that he never wanted to give up anything. It's not like you could go to him after a game and say, "Hey, Pete, you got four hits today. Can I have one of them to help me out a bit here?"

Pitcher **ROSS GRIMSLEY** *came up to the big club in 1971 and pitched three seasons for the Reds. He got a kick out of Rose's hustle:*

Why he did it, I have no idea. It's just what he did. One thing he would do is, if he got hit by a pitch, he would start running straight at the pitcher for a few steps and then peel off and keep on running down to first base. That was something. I can only imagine what the pitcher was thinking in a situation like that. It was just one more way of unnerving the other team, even in a small way.

DAVE BRISTOL *didn't just manage Rose one season in the minors, he also spent five seasons with him on the Reds:*

Pete never forgot a pitcher. A pitcher might get him out one way, and Pete would adjust. He had a short, compact swing that didn't get out of kilter very much.

To show you how much he matured over time, later on I asked him to go to the outfield (from second base) and he was adequate there. He played some left field and some right field.

When we got into the season, he would have to go serve some of his time in the army reserve during the daytime. That's when the coaches and I would wait at the ballpark until late afternoon for him to come by and work him out in the field and throw batting practice to him. Not a lot of players would have done that. But he came straight from the barracks to Crosley Field, and he went to work.

Pete wanted to win, and he wanted to get base hits. He was probably the greediest ballplayer I ever managed, as far as wanting to get a base hit. If he got one right off the bat, there was a good chance that he would go on and get five in the game. If he got two, he wanted three, and so on.

One time in Greenville (South Carolina), we were playing a doubleheader against the Dodgers' farm club—this was in '62—and he started off by going 0–for–2 in the first game, and he ended up going 5–for–7 for the day. He never gave up. At 0–for–2, that was killing him.

En route to winning the batting title in '68, he looked terrible on the Friday night of the last weekend of the season. I told him after Friday's game that, because we were playing a day game on Saturday, he should come to the ballpark twenty minutes earlier than usual so he could get some extra hitting in.

Gaylord Perry was pitching against us that day, and Pete started off going 4–for–4, on the fourth hit sliding into second for a double. Hal Lanier, who was playing second, said, "That's really something." And Pete said, "Yeah, that was my fourth hit." Lanier goes, "No, we've got the radio on in the dugout, and Matty Alou is 4–for–4 at Chicago. So Pete went up for a fifth time and got another base hit. The next day, Pete doubled off Ray Sadecki in the first inning, and I took him out and he won the batting title.

The next year, '69, we were in Atlanta playing our last game of the season. Somebody sitting in a box seat right near the dugout leaned out and said, "Pete, (Roberto) Clemente is 2–for–3 in Chicago. You need to get a base hit."

Clete Boyer was playing third base for the Braves. Pete went up and put down a perfect bunt down the third-base line that Boyer had no play on. That hit allowed Pete to win another batting title, this time beating out Clemente, and

I've still got that bat at home that Pete used to bunt to get that hit. He also gave me the bat with which he got his 3,999th hit.

-◁◯▷-

DAVE BRISTOL:

You just hoped you got to the ballpark before he did. He was always there early, wanting to improve. And he was always positive about it. It was always fun going to the ballpark knowing that Pete was going to be there, regardless of where I was with him, whether managing him at Macon or Cincinnati, coaching him at Philadelphia, or then working for him as a coach with the Reds in 1989.

I know about Pete Rose the ballplayer; the other part I don't know a damn thing about. I don't want to know.

-◁◯▷-

If Rose was selfish or greedy when it came to getting base hits, he gave up much of his time on the side to help people, especially when it came to mentoring others on how to play the game. GLENN SAMPLE, the former longtime baseball coach at the University of Cincinnati, can vouch for that:

I used to see him about every summer, because eventually I became the head baseball coach at the University of Cincinnati. I would take my team down to Florida every year to swing through and play some of the colleges down there.

I always worked it out so we would be able to make it to Tampa, for at least one day, where the Reds were going through spring training. We would work out with the Reds for one day, and that gave our players a chance to see how major-league camps were conducted. We were right out there with the team doing the drills, and sometimes we would play one of their satellite or Triple-A teams or somebody.

What really impressed me and my players was that Pete would be the first guy out for practice each time and the last guy to leave. Pete would come into the locker room and talk to our kids, and he would spend forty-five to sixty minutes talking about baseball. The guy was unbelievable, and he made so much sense, and he was talking without a prepared speech or whatever.

He would give instruction on things like how to bunt and when to go for the extra base, what to look for when you're ahead of the pitcher in the count. A lot of these were things that most college players had never heard before. Then, of course, he would talk about desire and hustle, and he would always work into his presentation some stories, such as what happened to him during his first couple years of minor-league ball.

⊞

GLENN SAMPLE:

Whenever I took my team down to meet the Reds for a day or two at spring training, I could see that they were moving people around a lot to different positions in the field.

One time after Pete had been moved to the outfield, we got to the field for our usual practice and there Pete was, already having somebody hit fungoes to him. He was in left field, and we had guys positioned around second and third base to take throws from the outfield.

Usually, the guys in the outfield throwing the ball in will just lob it back to the cutoff guy. Not Pete, he played *every* ball hit to him like it was a sacrifice fly and there were men on second and third tagging up. On every one of those fungoes, Pete would backpedal a bit and then come in a few steps to make the catch and unload the ball to the cutoff man or one of the guys at second or third, simulating trying to throw a guy out.

He didn't have a really good arm, but he was accurate. He would throw and throw and throw—on one bounce to second, then on one bounce to third, and then to home. It doesn't surprise me that, after converting to the outfield, Pete one season led the National League in assists by an outfielder.

Pete never let up. A lot of guys who have made it to the majors won't even go after fungoes that aren't hit right to them. Too many guys are there worrying about hitting home runs without showing any real concern for throwing guys out. Not Pete. This one time, he was doing this full tilt for about thirty minutes, only working on plays from the outfield.

Pete was the ultimate example to our guys of how to play and how to hustle.

-❊-

SAMPLE *also addresses Rose's aggressive base running:*

The other thing about Pete was that he wasn't overly fast. He ranged somewhere from fair to good, but when it came to going from first to third, there were few base runners as good as or better than Pete

When he got up to bat, he always knew exactly where the outfielders were playing him. If he saw, as soon as the ball left the bat, that there was a possibility of the ball getting into the gap, he would be ready to go for the extra base. He had catalogued these guys as to their tendencies and whether they were left-handed or right-handed. If an outfielder had to throw across his body in getting the ball back to the infield—such as a right-handed right fielder chasing down a ball toward the right foul line, Pete already knew that the opportunity was there for him to get the extra base.

He would stretch more singles into doubles than any-body else I ever saw. He loved to challenge guys, even to get them to make a hard throw when he had no intent of going for second. He knew every player and his position, and he also was a good bunter. He kept defenses on their toes.

As a kid growing up in Cincinnati, you see a ballplayer like that and you want to be like him. You've also got to be careful about trying to emulate some ballplayers too closely. I remember a lot of guys my age trying to copy Willie Mays's basket catch, and many times we would end up dropping the ball.

Rose also made quite an impression on at least one opposing player, that being future Rose antagonist **BUD HARRELSON,** *a shortstop with the New York Mets. Harrelson:*

When I came up as a rookie in 1966, I remember playing against the Reds with guys like Rose and (Tommy) Helms already there. Here I was, a middle infielder, too, and they watched me. Before the second game I played against them, they walked over to me and talked to me a little bit about a couple of things.

I forgot exactly what they said, except I remember that I was pretty much in awe, first of all, that they would even take an interest in me. When they walked away, I thought, *You know, they didn't have to do that.* I guess they saw this lit-tle scrappy guy out there trying hard, getting the bat knocked out of his hands a lot—I was just learning how to switch-hit.

When you see guys like that talking to you and trying to help you grow as a player, I thought, *I would expect veterans on my own ball club to do that, but not players on an opposing team.* That's when the game was kind of simple. Just go play. Without all the money issues.

❈

HARRELSON, *on the Charlie Hustle bit. Harrelson later would be a Rose teammate, with the Phillies in 1979:*

He was old school. I hustled a lot, too. I was intense, as he was, but he was probably less nervous than I was in terms of tension.

He played hard, and he was that way in Philly, too, although he was getting on toward the end of his career. He would often go from first to third on a base hit, and he didn't give a crap about how good any of the outfielders threw. He just had great instincts.

Pete would probably hate for me to say this, but in a way he could be compared to Sophia Loren. It's that everything-being-in-the-right-place kind of thing. Pete wasn't fast but he ran hard. He got a lot of singles but didn't steal a lot of bases. He didn't hit the ball with a lot of power, usually, but he did have power. You wouldn't consider him a home-run hitter. He didn't have a great arm. He just did everything he had to do to be successful.

I don't know, maybe Sophia Loren is not the best analogy. But think about it. If you look at her closely, you might even think that she's not really that beautiful. You might regard her nose as being a bit too long or a little big, and this and that, but the whole is greater than the sum of her parts. I mean, look at her. Everything works together. Her beauty is mind-boggling.

There are so many names in the game that we can consider as underachievers. Here's a guy, Rose, who obviously was at the top of his game for a very long time, but when you broke it down into individual skills, you wondered why.

❈

PHOTO COURTESY OF CINCINNATI REDS

A hustling Rose was always ready with a headfirst slide, even going into home.

JACK BALDSCHUN *talks about pitching against Rose:*

Pete didn't ever hurt me much. He was a Punch-and-Judy type hitter to me. He'd slap at the ball, hit it anywhere. Mainly, his deal was just to get the ball started going somewhere, usually on the ground, and then run like hell. That was his main objective—just to hit the ball on the ground.

Pete never really was a power hitter in the days that I pitched against him. He was a slap hitter, slapping it in the other direction just trying to get a base hit. If you pitched in on him, he could pull it, and he had a little bit of power there, batting left-handed. Still, he never hurt me that much.

Pete would slide headfirst a lot, and he thought that would get him to the base a little faster, and I suppose it did. But I don't like what he did to Ray Fosse, not at all. It's one thing to play the game hard, but in an All-Star Game? If it had been the last game of the World Series, that's a different story. I don't go for a lot of stuff that Pete did.

ED BRINKMAN, Rose's former teammate at Western Hills High, knew Pete well enough to know that he shouldn't have been surprised by anything Rose accomplished in the majors:

It didn't surprise me that he was leading the National League in hitting by the late sixties. What did surprise me was how he was hitting around .330 in the minors right after he had signed—that made an impression on me, like "Wow! What has he done to get these kinds of numbers?" By the time he was hitting that well in the major leagues, I already knew that he had gotten over the hump.

His longevity might have surprised me somewhat, staying healthy for that long and getting two hundred hits a season for all those years. Not that I didn't think Pete took good care of himself—he did. It's just that those numbers are so unbelievable—for *anybody!*

JACK BALDSCHUN saw Rose as a self-made man:

There wasn't a lot of teaching going on in the majors, so a lot of what you did to improve, you had to do on your own.

Pete was not one of those guys in the clubhouse who would go around trying to fire other guys up. His mind was on other things when he got off the field. He wasn't much of a teammate. He chummed around with Tommy Helms, but that's about it.

KAROLYN ROSE offers her take on her ex-husband's down-to-the-wire batting titles in 1968 and 1969:

Those back-to-back batting titles in 1968 and 1969 were unbelievable. When he did that, I made the statement that I would be the first woman to sleep with the back-to-back batting champion, and what a thrill that would be for me.

I always got a kick out of it when he hit home runs, only because he never hit that many. If he hit twelve home runs in one season, I'd think, "Oh, my God, that's really good."

GEORGE CULVER *revisits Rose's batting title in 1968 and how he edged out Matty Alou:*

Dave Bristol came to us before the last game (after Rose had gone 5–for–5 on Saturday) and said that there would be no batting practice before the game, unless someone wanted to take it. And there Pete was, the only guy on the team taking batting practice that day, and he did it for about twenty to thirty minutes. I mean this is the 162nd game of the season, the last day of the season, and there's Pete out there taking his full complement of cuts on a Sunday morning.

Going back to the day before, we were playing the Giants, and Gaylord Perry was pitching for them, while Alou was going against the Cubs, who had Ferguson Jenkins on the mound. So it would be Rose versus Perry and Alou versus Jenkins. Our game was starting an hour before the Cubs game, so this would give Pete a chance to get a head start on Alou.

Pete's first time up, Perry threw one of his spitters and that really got Pete riled up. Pete ended up getting a base hit and then got a hit his next time up, making him 2–for–2. Sometime after that the public-address announcer came on to announce that Alou had gotten a hit his first time up in that other game. We all looked over at Pete, and we could see the juices really starting to kick in.

Next time up, Pete got another hit. Now he's 3–for–3. A few minutes later we hear that Alou has gotten his second hit and now is 2–for–2. On and on it went.

His fifth time up, Pete dragged a bunt and beat it out to first for his fifth hit of the game: 5–for–5. We then heard that Alou had popped out or something his next time up. He ended up going 3–for–5. It was one of the most amazing things I had ever seen. I just sat there watching this, thinking how incredible this guy is. Yeah, when you looked at him standing there, he didn't look like a baseball player, but his mind was totally on baseball. He was always like one of those little kids who just chew the game up.

ROSS GRIMSLEY *remembers how Rose would always try to fire up others around him, beseeching them to get on base, too:*

Every time he was leading off, it didn't matter who was pitching, Pete would come back to the bench, if he had made an out, look back at the pitcher, and scream at the top of his lungs, "Nothin'! He ain't got nothin'!" And he would yell this regardless of what he had done at the plate. Nolan Ryan could have been pitching and throwing three hundred miles an hour, and Pete still would have come back screaming the same thing. "He ain't got nothin'!"

GRIMSLEY *continues:*

In spring training, he would wear the batting-practice pitchers out. Whatever he did, he would always do it to the max. He would hit in the cage until his hands were bleeding from blisters. Then he would go inside, wrap them up with some tape, and go back out and hit some more. I never saw anyone else do it quite like that, and sometimes I would be thinking, *Hey, enough is enough.* He would hit and hit and keep on hitting.

Pete was also great at being able to stick the bat out there and foul balls off until he got the pitch he wanted. It was amazing how he did it, to get the pitch he liked. As an opposing pitcher—and I did pitch against him some after I got to the Expos—all you could hope for that he would hit the ball at someone so you would have a chance at getting him out. Your best hope was to get him to chase a bad pitch.

— ✥ —

Any list of top-ten Pete Rose memories has to include the time he barreled into catcher RAY FOSSE, scoring from second on a Jim Hickman single, to give the National League a 5–4 victory in the 1970 All-Star Game—at Cincinnati's Riverfront Stadium, no less. Fosse recounts the play at the plate:

A lot of things were going through my mind when I was waiting for (Amos) Otis's throw. This wasn't an ordinary ball game. The president of the United States (Richard Nixon) had thrown out the first ball. I was young, just twenty-three. I was playing with guys like Frank Robinson and Harmon Killebrew, tremendous names to me.

There's a bad play a catcher can make in that situation. The *Olé!* Shot. Get out of the way. The runner goes by like a charging bull and you wave a tag at him, like a matador. That's the wrong play. The right play is block the plate. I knew sixty-five million people were watching on TV. Aside from that, I wanted the respect of my peers. I wasn't going to look like a fool and get out of the way. I was the Cleveland catcher, not the San Diego Chicken.[13]

— ✥ —

Author JAMES RESTON JR. had this to write regarding the aftermath of Fosse's injury, which basically, although not immediately, brought a promising career to ruin:

For several days, Rose nursed a badly bruised thigh before he returned to the lineup. Fosse was not as lucky. In terrible pain, he had been rushed to a hospital, where he was x-rayed and told that his collarbone was severely bruised but not broken or fractured. . . . Fosse was back in uniform several days later, slated by his manager, Alvin Dark, to catch the Cleveland ace, Sam McDowell. When he took batting practice, however, he found that he could scarcely swing the bat. He had no power in his swing, and he could not lift his left arm higher than his shoulder. When he told Dark about the problem, the manager sloughed it off. "Don't worry about offense," Dark said. "Just handle the pitchers."

The spirit of those times, before the age of huge contracts, was different than it is today. If a player said he was hurt but couldn't prove it, he was expected to play. If he complained, he risked acquiring the label "Jake" for faking an injury. He was paid to play. Dutifully, Fosse took his cortisone shots and obeyed Dark's order.[14]

Rose's hustling extended from between the lines to between the sheets, as over time he would practically flaunt a girlfriend in front of his wife, fiancée, or another girlfriend. **EARL LAWSON,** *legendary Cincinnati sportswriter, once had this to say in advising Rose to cool it with the extramarital affairs:*

This is the late sixties. I said to him, "Damn it, watch the fooling around. I know you're going to fool around on the road, but at home your wife is going to realize that she's becoming the laughingstock of the community. And she may still love you, but just to salvage her pride she's going to have to tell you to get lost." But that didn't make it. He didn't listen. A woman has her pride. I tried to make Pete understand that.

Pete would listen to me about some things, especially when he was younger. But even then, if it was something he didn't want to hear, he wouldn't. When I talked to him about not cheating at home, it was like telling him "Don't eat candy." It was like, "But I like candy, Daddy." "Well, then, go ahead and eat it. It'll make you sick, it'll give you bad teeth, but go ahead." He was advised, but he chose to ignore it.[15]

KAROLYN ROSE, *Pete's first wife, had this to say about being a baseball wife, which she was for more than fifteen years:*

It had its ups and downs. With me, it really wasn't anything different. I always considered myself Karolyn Rose, not "Pete Rose's wife." That's one of the reasons why, I think, that I could go to a ballpark and everybody would say hello to me. They knew me for myself, not just as Pete's wife.

KAROLYN ROSE *weighs in on the best and worst parts of being married to Pete:*

He gave me two beautiful kids (daughter Fawn and son Pete Jr.). I thank him and the good Lord for that.

The worst part? The women. That's the worst thing he could ever do to me. The funny part about it is that I knew everything that was going on. I didn't have to go out of my house to find out what he was doing. I lived in Cincinnati, after all. I think it's fair to say that there are many people in Cincinnati who love me, and maybe they were afraid of my being hurt. I don't know if they were trying to protect me or what, but I was able to learn about everything.

If I could have kept my kids little the rest of their lives, I would probably still be married to him because then I would have been able to handle that other side of Pete. I told him when he went on the road, "If you find someone else much better than me, then you make sure you make a phone call, because I'm not coming over to the airport to pick you up." That was my standing joke with him.

As the sixties drew to a close, things were about to change with the Reds. Bob Howsam fired the likable Dave Bristol and brought in a prematurely gray unknown who would prove to be, perhaps, the most vital part of the team that would soon become known as the Big Red Machine. That was **SPARKY ANDERSON,** *who came on the scene and didn't stop with the Rose shuffle among positions in the field:*

He would play anywhere. Even if he wasn't the most dynamic player at a position, he would play it if you asked him to, and would play it the hardest that he could play it.

ANDERSON, *on rating Rose in terms of baseball's great players:*

He's the toughest competitor I've ever seen in my lifetime, but keep in mind I was in baseball "only" forty-four years. To steal a phrase from (Tommy) Lasorda, "He would compete at you from nighttime to nighttime, and the next night, if it took that." That's the way he was.

I said to him one time, "You think that you're eighteen years old." He said, "Skip, I will always be eighteen years old."

People say that Pete did this and Pete did that, but don't let any one of us go to the mirror and think that we didn't do this or didn't do that. We've all done something. For more than twenty years, I don't think anyone who went to watch a game in which Pete played felt like they had blown their money.

I'm not in any way applauding what Pete might have done, but don't get to throwing rocks at him, because that rock might get you, too. He gave on the field as much as any man has ever given. He should be in the Hall of Fame. Now I can understand why he might not be allowed to do anything more (in terms of an official baseball capacity), but he must be in Cooperstown. That's what that place is for. That place is there for records—it wasn't made for Johnny Doolittle to walk into.

3

The Big Red Machine

It doesn't qualify as a dynasty. It lasted less than a decade, and there were no threepeats. Those shortcomings aside, it's okay to say that the Cincinnati Reds from 1970 through 1978 were one of the greatest baseball teams in history. During that span, with Sparky Anderson at the helm, the Reds won five divisional titles, four National League pennants, and two World Series titles. Their success forged an era much shorter than that of the great New York Yankees teams yet longer than the spurt the dynamic Oakland A's put together in the seventies.

Getting picky, we could say that the term *Big Red Machine* came in vogue only after the back-to-back World Series championships of 1975 and 1976. Retrospect allows us to fudge a little bit and broaden the the era of the Big Red

Machine to 1970–78, because the likes of Rose, Johnny Bench, Dave Concepcion, and Sparky Anderson were common threads through all nine of those seasons. Tony Perez was there for the first seven years, George Foster for the last eight, and Joe Morgan for the last six.

Five of those team members now reside in baseball's Hall of Fame. Perhaps Rose will make it six some day.

Wanna start an argument? Try making the case that one of those guys was the key cog to the Big Red Machine's success. Bench? Great catcher, super arm, terrific hitter, a pair of MVPs. Morgan? Solid second baseman, base-stealing master, terrific hitter, team leader, a pair of MVPs. Perez? Rose? Anderson? Take your pick and give it a shot.

Between 1970 and 1979, Sparky Anderson's Reds averaged ninety-six victories a year, and they did all this with only one twenty-game winner the whole time. That was Jim Merritt, who squeaked by in 1970 with a 20–12 record.

Those guys were good.

❦

Sparky Anderson had managed a minor-league team in Toronto and served as a coach with the Reds' Triple-A farm club in San Diego before taking the manager's job in Cincinnati in 1970—after he had accepted a position with the California Angels. Pitcher JACK BALDSCHUN:

I was with Sparky Anderson when he was with San Diego, and I remember him saying, "Boy, I'd love to have my hands on that team over there." When he got (to the Reds), he just let them play.

❦

Under SPARKY ANDERSON, the Reds took off, winning seventy of their first hundred games en route to running away with the National League West title.

Anderson recalls the nice situation he walked into in
Cincinnati:

As a coach in San Diego, I had seen them play the year before. After I got the job, I called the coaches and I said, "I've seen this club, and we'll win by ten [games] or more."

I don't know if any other team has ever done this, but we broke camp that year with eight rookies. We had (Bernie) Carbo, (Hal) McRae, (Darrel) Chaney, (Dave) Concepcion, (Wayne) Simpson, (Don) Gullett, (Ross) Grimsley, and (Frank) Duffy. I defy any other team to show me when they ever broke camp with eight rookies. I told my boss, Bob Howsam, "Look, we don't need these old guys. Why don't we get them out of here? And let's go with these kids." There was nothing brilliant about it; I just knew we had to get these young guys in there.

One thing we did was to platoon Carbo and McRae in left field. I think they ended up averaging something like .318 between them at the plate. Then we had (Bobby) Tolan in center and Rose in right. When you stop and think about it, they talk about how we became known as the Big Red Machine, when at that time we were the Little Red Machine. They were all kids.

Bob Howsam, our general manager, probably did as good a job at putting a team together as we'll ever see in the history of baseball. He knew how to place people, and he made the promise that "We will never trade a young guy for an old guy to try and win a pennant."

One thing about that club, after it became the Big Red Machine, is that there weren't just one or two guys who were the top dogs leading everyone else around. They all liked each other, and they loved the game of baseball. They didn't worry about things like who the leader was. I hear this stuff today being said about how some guy "is great in the clubhouse," and I have to ask what is he doing in there, because

I would like to know. Hey, if you've got a guy who is such a great clubhouse leader, then maybe you oughtta get rid of the manager. He's useless.

-=❂=-

*Reds General Manager **BOB HOWSAM**, on what Anderson's arrival in Cincinnati in 1970 meant to the ballclub:*

When I went over to Cincinnati in 1967, the team was still at Crosley Field. It was a ballpark with a lot of charm, but it was such that we still needed to move into a new one.

At that time, the organization didn't have the kind of scouting system that I thought would work best for them. So many changes were needed, and made. Dave Bristol was a fine fellow, but after being there a few years, I felt that he had reached his level as to how far he could take our ballclub.

In 1970 I brought in Sparky Anderson, who had done a very fine job as manager at Asheville (North Carolina) and then as a third-base coach at our Triple-A team in San Diego. When I hired him, he was going to the California Angels to be a coach. Sparky was a fine young manager who was willing to work. He was a terrific fit for our ballclub.

We won the National League West by about twenty games and went on to play Baltimore in the World Series. I really believed that we had better ballplayers than the Orioles did, but our guys were all young. Late in the season, I tried to get Ron Fairly from the Dodgers, because he was someone who had been around and had gone through a few World Series with a wonderful organization. But I couldn't work out a deal to get him.

-=❂=-

HOWSAM *offers some interesting insights about the Reds' home park:*

When I got to Cincinnati, we were just a few years away from going into a new stadium (Riverfront), which had AstroTurf, and I believed in AstroTurf and I still do, for a number of reasons. Let me just say that it makes the game very interesting.

It rained a lot in Cincinnati along the Ohio River. What it does is come in in the late afternoon, like around six or six-thirty. It pours for about an hour, and then it's just gone. If you didn't have a surface you could play on under circumstances like that, then you were in danger of losing a ballgame. With the AstroTurf at Riverfront, we only lost one game (to the weather) in Cincinnati. That gave us the opportunity to keep the momentum of winning going, because we weren't getting interrupted by rainouts.

Now they have a lot of new grasses that they can use, and it will be interesting to see how the new stadium in Cincinnati works out, because it has grass.

Most people following teams don't think about this kind of stuff, and maybe it sounds kind of strange to even be talking about it, but when you're operating a ballclub, you understand this kind of reasoning very well.

In coming to the Reds, one of the first things Sparky Anderson did was chat with Pete Rose a little bit, with Rose being one of the few veterans he was willing to keep in an ongoing turnover of talent. **ANDERSON:**

I got along great with Pete. He and I talked all the time. He was a tough guy, and I like a guy that is tough and brings it right forward to you, straight up. I don't like that little weasel-type guy.

He told me that he made the most money on the ballclub, and that if I had any problems that I should go to him, and that anytime I wanted to use him as a set-up in a meeting, to go ahead and do it. "Rip me up good," he said, "because then everyone will go, 'Oh, man, he's rippin' him up good, I'd better watch out.'"

I had street shtick, and I can understand people pretty quickly, knowing if they're trying to con me or whatever. If you try to con me, you've lost the moment you open your mouth. Even my mom use to tell me how I always seemed to be studying people, that I was always interested in knowing more about them.

My forte is watching people in a restaurant or in an airport. I love to watch how ignorant people are in a restaurant. I was great at reading body language, and Pete's body language said to me that old saying, "You ain't going to ask for no quarters, but you're not going to get any either." To me, that's the way everybody should be when they're into athletics. Why back off when going after someone? You bowl over them. I always felt that the way he did it was the absolute right way.

✦

ANDERSON *offers a bit of introspection:*

I was a Jekyll and Hyde as a manager. Away from the field, I never took anything too seriously, and I wanted the clubhouse to be a place of fun. But once I got to the dugout, I was pretty serious about the game.

When I first walked in there, I was only thirty-five years old, and because of that, I said the first step I'm going to take is to name the hometown boy (Rose) as captain. That's the kind of decision that comes from the street, see. If you have street smarts, you know where you've got to make your first plug in the dam. And I plugged up the dam real quick. I always used to say, you get your four top guys and put them in your pocket and keep them there, and then everything will work out.

Pete is a guy who came in expecting to do one thing—win. He doesn't come for anything else but for that, and he's not going to get into anyone else's business. He was going to take care of his own business and make sure that he was ready to play. I don't remember ever meeting another competitor like that in my life-

PHOTO COURTESY OF CINCINNATI REDS

As evidenced by this pitcher's-eye view, Rose's hunched-over stance and compact swing were the source of nightmares for many National League hurlers during the 1970s.

time. That's just the way he was. He and (Joe) Morgan used to do a lot of jabbering, and Tony Perez as well. But Tony was kind of like the overseer; he could keep everybody under wraps. He was also a good instigator, someone who could get things going.

ANDERSON *talks about the young players he started bringing into the Reds' fold in 1970, including the task of trying to piece together a pitching staff that was neither deep nor experienced:*

Wayne Simpson really was dynamic and had a great arm, but the unexpected surprise was how Carbo and McRae gave us more production than we had thought they would. It also helped that we were able to bring Davey Concepcion along slowly, because we also had Woody Woodward and Darrel Chaney able to play shortstop. We had the luxury of being able to pick our spots for Dave and bring him along slowly, not letting him go against the Bob Gibsons of the world in that first season. We could afford to do that.

Jimmy Merritt pitched well for us. Even though he had a high ERA, he always kept us in the game. And Gary Nolan was sensational, coming off an arm injury. Then (Don) Gullett just exploded. Our plan was to start out by babying him along, but all of a sudden he just came on. One rule I made with Gullett was that he would never have to face the winning run while leading after seven innings, and I always stuck to that.

I've heard it said that I supposedly did a pretty good job of handling pitchers, but I have to credit Al Lopez and Charlie Dressen for that. Al was living in Tampa, and I got to talk to him many times. I asked him one time what he had always considered to be the main thing about managing. He said, "One thing, Sparky. I never take my eyes off the visiting pitcher and never took my eyes off of my pitcher. They will expose themselves if you keep your eyes on them—they will tell you when they're done."

Even though he's a Hall of Famer and all that, Al Lopez never has received the recognition that he deserves. He was a brilliant manager.

⊞

*In 1971 the Reds fell apart early, losing Bobby Tolan to injury for the season, and were sixteen games out of first by the end of May. The Reds played better in the second half of the season, winning more than half of their games, but could finish no better than fifth place. That's when **BOB HOWSAM** made his biggest move, one that would bring together key components of the*

*Big Red Machine. He forged a multi-player deal with
the Astros that included sending Rose's longtime pal
Tommy Helms and first baseman Lee May to Houston
for several players, including second baseman Joe
Morgan and pitcher Jack Billingham. Howsam:*

When I made the trade, I told our people, "We have given
Houston the pennant, but we needed these players for the
future."

We got five players there, including Joe Morgan, which
turned out to be a wonderful deal for us. Geronimo turned
out to be an outstanding outfielder, Denis Menke played
some great third base for us, and Jack Billingham won nineteen games for us a couple of times.

We went on to win and gradually became the Big Red
Machine. Even when we were down in the ninth inning, we
still thought we were going to win the ballgame. It was very
gratifying to know that everyone in our organization had a
hand in putting all this together and that it led to some
world championships for us.

This wasn't the first time I had put my neck out on
trades involving popular players. Back in the sixties, while I
was with the Saint Louis Cardinals, I traded away Ken Boyer,
Bill White, and Dick Groat, but we had some nice young
players coming up and we needed room for them. And then
we got Orlando Cepeda and Roger Maris. By the time I left
to go to the Reds, I had a club in Saint Louis all signed up
and ready to go, and they went on to play in the World
Series two years in a row, winning in 1967.

That's how you build a successful ballclub—you build
for the future. You have to go out and do the things you
think are right, and don't look back. That's what we did with
the Reds, and it paid off. We set out to give Cincinnati what
I thought they wanted—an All-American type of team, right
down to the rule of no facial hair.

As much as he liked playing for the Reds, TOMMY HELMS said he had few regrets about being traded to the Astros:

That trade actually helped Houston, because that became the first time they had ever finished as high as second. I wasn't disappointed by the trade, because I thought we could win in Houston. I thought we had the players to do it. Besides, you had no choice back then—you went wherever they sent you, because this was all before things like free agency. You had a bossman back then.

Big Red Machine catcher JOHNNY BENCH, on Rose:

He's the most selfish player I've ever known—and we need eight more just like him.[1]

ROSS GRIMSLEY was one among several young arms who came up to the Reds in the early seventies, and he spent three seasons pitching for Sparky Anderson before moving on:

When I first came up, I thought it was kind of neat how the veteran players like Bench, Rose, and Perez would watch over us young guys. They'd give us just enough rope to hang ourselves but then would reel us back in. It was a pretty good friendship.

This was at the very beginnings of the Big Red Machine, and at the time there was a big changeover going on with the pitching staff. Guys like Milt Wilcox, Wayne Simpson, Don Gullett, and me were just coming along. We struggled in '71 after having won the World Series in '70, then '72 was the gung-ho year in which we went to the World Series against Oakland.

These guys knew they were good and that they were going to win, but as far as showing off about it or having any sort of swagger, there wasn't any of that. We knew we could score runs—that wasn't a problem. The main concern was holding the other team down, because we still weren't a real good pitching team.

The pitchers hated Sparky, and he hated us. "Captain Hook," we called him. He was really quick to make a change. We were really looking over our shoulders half the time, wondering when he was going to take us out of the game. Sparky's pitchers were kind of like the punters and placekickers in football—you don't notice them until they've blown a kick or two. Sparky's philosophy was to make the eight starting guys happy, and the rest of them, to hell with 'em. It worked, obviously. You keep your horses happy, and you have a good chance. Then you just roll.

⚬

The more time **SPARKY ANDERSON** *spent around Rose, the more he thought he could see through some of Charlie Hustle's off-the-field tactics:*

I remember when Rose wanted a raise and decided to hold out before the 1971 season:

I wasn't ever worried about Pete's holding out. In those days, you had two types of ballplayers—those who wanted to go through spring training and those who didn't. After the tough spring training we had had in 1970, Pete didn't want to go through the whole thing the next year.

Guys would hold out on purpose and maybe miss the first ten days, and then they were on their own to get in shape because the (exhibition) games were starting. What the Latin guys would do is say that they were having trouble getting their visas, when they had had several months during the offseason to get that stuff taken care of. It didn't take me long to figure out that they didn't want to be there either. They were in no hurry.

A holdout then wasn't always about dollars. It was more that they just wanted to miss a little time. Pete used to come to camp in pretty good shape anyway. Funny thing with him: He never worked out as far as I knew, in terms of going to the gym or lifting weights. He was so strong, it was unbelievable. He had the strongest hands that I have ever gripped. It was from swinging the bat; he was always swinging a bat.

He had a thing with me, that as soon as he was ready in the spring, he would want both a right-hander and a left-hander to throw batting practice to him. Joe Nuxhall, the former pitcher-turned-radio-announcer, was the left-hander, and the right-hander was Scott Braden, our minor-league pitching coach. About two weeks into camp, maybe a hair longer, Pete would say, "I'm ready," and I knew exactly what he meant.

After a game or after a workout, we would set it up over at the minor-league camp for Joe and Scott to pitch to Pete. Joe would throw fifteen pitches and then Scott would throw fifteen. Pete had this bottle of liquid, a skin toughener, that he kept in the batting cage with him. He would bat lefty against Scott and righty against Joe, and all the time he would be putting this stuff on his hands, making his hands tougher. That's one of the reasons why, come August 1, that pitchers would be tired and Pete wasn't.

I call him an animal because he was one of those guys who could go all day. He loves the game, he likes the rough and tough part of it, he loves competing, and he loves to win. Many times guys would tell me, "He's a selfish player who only cares about himself and how many hits he gets." I once said, "Let me tell you something, and don't you ever forget this: You give me eight players on that field as selfish as him, and you'll never lose a game."

You have to be selfish to go get it. They're not going to ask someone else to get it for them. To my knowledge, Pete never asked nobody, ever, to do anything for him.

ANDERSON elaborates on the era of the Big Red Machine:

It was a wonderful thing to live through. It was a name that just stuck and has remained through time. People ask me, "How did it feel to be around Johnny Bench, Pete Rose, and all those guys?" And I'll say, "Wait a minute, hold the phone. When you're working at something like this, you don't even think about that stuff. You don't think, *That's Johnny Bench, that's Pete Rose, and that's Joe Morgan.* You're at work. You don't think about who they are, but you say to yourself, *That's my catcher, that's my first baseman, and that's my second baseman.* There's no time to stand back and admire this. Isn't it funny that we're all just human.

It has to rate among the five best teams in baseball history. Where people want to put us, I don't know. I don't know if we're number one, number three, or what. I didn't get to see the '27 Yankees or any of those great Dodgers teams. I saw one of those great Baltimore Orioles teams only once (in the 1970 World Series), and I know that the Oakland A's had a nice run. All I can say is that it was one of the five best. Plus, I had never seen a team that was more professional-*acting* on the airplane, in the clubhouse, or on the field.

I had seen all the other teams in the league, and I knew that when we came on the field, there was something different about us from all the rest. I think it was a lot of arrogance, and I don't mean that in a bad way. It was a good arrogance in that they had tremendous pride in themselves and they knew how to act. I don't remember anything ever being said or reported about that team that involved detrimental or unprofessional behavior. Like Johnny Bench. There were times he would come to me and say, "You know, I don't agree with you on this, but if that's how you want me to do it, then that's the way I'll do it."

Those guys knew that they were ballplayers; that was their job. They did what you asked them to do, and they did it the best they could. And there's no question that they had great talent. Beyond that, they were really good people. And when the game was on, they were really into the game. When they got dressed into their uniforms, they were different people, and when they went out the clubhouse door and out onto the field, they were going to take care of business.

Another thing I liked about them is that they never cried or alibied after a loss. None of this whining stuff. It's like they were saying, "Okay, so we got beat. We'll be back here to play those guys again, same time tomorrow."

⟨⟩

ROSS GRIMSLEY, on team leadership with the Reds:

Rose and Perez were the two guys who ran most of the show in the clubhouse, especially Perez. There were times that Morgan would be pouting about something, and they would be all over him. It was pretty fun sometimes. It was a fun team to be a part of because everyone knew what their job was. The place pretty much ran itself, and I can't remember there ever being any real problems.

One of the ways in which Pete was a team leader was in how hard he worked. You saw him doing all this, and you figured you ought to at least be doing some of it. And it rubbed off somewhat on other players. You don't see that as much now. The only guys you see really working are the guys who don't have as much talent and probably aren't going anywhere. Still, in all the years I played, I can't think of anyone who approached Rose in terms of work ethic. There's no one I would even put in the same category.

PHOTO COURTESY OF CINCINNATI REDS

With all the titles, pennants, and championships the Big Red Machine won during the 1970s, there were plenty of chances for someone to get carried off the field.

You can't take away what he did as a player. He made himself into a good player. He wasn't particularly fast and didn't have a great arm, but he was a bit of a showman, too. He knew people liked seeing him hustle. He became a good player, but he was a good entertainer as well who could make people happy.

BOB HOWSAM *remembers an unsung hero, or two, from the Big Red Machine days:*

Dave Concepcion never really got the recognition that he deserved, and neither did Cesar Geronimo, who was a great centerfielder.

In the near quarter-century that Rose played major-league ball, there were about a half-dozen "Reds-letter days" that defined the career of Charlie Hustle. One was the Ray Fosse collision. Another was the second-base scuffle with Mets shortstop Bud Harrelson in a 1973 National League Championship Series game at Shea Stadium, after a sliding Rose had gone hard into second, swiping Harrelson while trying to break up a double play. Tempers soared and benches cleared. **SPARKY ANDERSON** *remembers:*

Yeah, he went in and hit Harrelson hard, but he hit him clean. He didn't hit him with his spikes up or anything like that. He just hit him good and hard and clean.

The way I understand it, Bud called him something pretty good. Pete wasn't going to buy that. He pushed him hard, and if he had wanted to, he would have disintegrated him. But he didn't.

The biggest problem came in the immediate aftermath of that scuffle, with the guys running up there and taking cheap shots. By then, Pete and Bud were done with their thing—it was just like two brothers being in a quick wrestling match, and then it's over.

Bud Harrelson's a terrific person and Pete really respected him, and I know Bud respected Pete. It wouldn't have been much of anything had it not been for all the other stuff and the cheap shots. And one of them came from our side (Pedro Borbon), so it wasn't a matter of just the Mets giving out cheap shots. We had our share, too. I was out there, scared that one of my own guys was going to pop me, because those are the guys who hate you the most.

I give the New York fans credit because they can get really excited, but sometimes they get too wild. That incident gave them an alibi to really get carried away.

ROSS GRIMSLEY, *a Reds pitcher, was there, too:*

It was kind of scary at Shea. They had to move the Reds players' wives away from the dugout because fans were starting to get really irate. It was awful. Matter of fact, the big concern was how they were going to get Rose off the field when the game was over. They told the rest of us players to grab a bat and put a helmet on. The police were telling us that.

When the game ended, people started coming out of the stands and jumping over the dugout—it looked like a waterfall of people coming off of the dugout roof. One thing I remember is that after Darrel Chaney had grabbed a bat, some guy jumped on his back. Darrel shook the guy off of him and then took a full swing, whacking the guy in the leg. Somehow the guy jumped up and ran off. Either he had a tough leg or Darrel had a pretty poor swing, one of the two.

While all this was going in, they managed to get Rose off the field and into the clubhouse. But we still had trouble later on trying to get onto the team bus. People were throwing bottles and rocks at us. It was a mess. At that ballpark, you never knew what those fans were going to do.

BUD HARRELSON *offers some background that helps to explain his battle with Rose:*

A lot of people seem to remember my career from the standpoint of that one incident. But, granted, it was a playoff game. National TV.

We had been in Cincinnati earlier in the series, when Jon Matlack threw the game of his life against the Big Red Machine. They had trouble making contact, and the game was over. My misfortune is that Jon was lockered next to me. All the writers were about six deep around our lockers.

Some guy turns to me and asks, "What did you think about the Big Red Machine against Jon Matlack today?" I said, "They all looked like me hitting." Well, somebody obviously went back to the Reds clubhouse and put the word out, although I didn't know anything about that.

The next day we were working out at Shea Stadium, where the series would continue. I thought what I had said was one of those "funny, ha-ha" things. But something got lost in the translation. After a while, Joe Morgan comes walking over to me and says, "If you ever say that about me again . . ." And I said, "What? What are you talking about? I didn't say anything about you."

Rusty Staub is standing right there, listening to all this. It just so happens I knew Joe. We had both grown up in the San Francisco Bay Area. But he grabbed me by the shirt, at which time Rusty intervened, saying, "You know, Joe, Bud didn't say a damn thing. I don't know what's going on here either." Joe apologized, but then he told us, "Pete is going to use this to fire up the ballclub, then he's going to come after you."

I told Pete when it happened that it was a cheap-shot play at second, and that's when he got up and hit me. It got over pretty fast, and the rest is history. The outskirts of that were probably more interesting, such as Pedro Borbon's biting a hole out of Buzz Capra's cap. There was some funny stuff.

Writers were looking for me after the game, but I was hiding out in the training room. I finally came out and kind of pooh-poohed it, saying some funny stuff about how my brother used to beat me up, too. There was no way I was going to say that I should have kicked his butt.

HARRELSON *continues:*

I wanted to hit him only because I was so ticked, but before I could even do anything, he grabbed me by the shirt and physically lifted me off the ground. You know how hard it is to hit somebody when you've got your feet off the ground?

I still have the utmost respect for the way the guy played the game. And I played with him in 1979 with Philadelphia. I signed late and wasn't there when Pete got there. Then (Larry) Bowa broke his finger or something like that, and I called them and they brought me back. I had been there in '78, but I hadn't retired. I was playing softball, and because I still weighed only 150 pounds, it didn't take me long to get back into playing shape. At the time, I was in Baltimore doing some color commentary for some college games, so it was an easy drive up there for me.

I enjoyed playing with Pete that year. He was a real pro, and I was able to play out the season with the Phils, helping them out a little bit.

With **SPARKY ANDERSON** *at the helm, the Reds played in five World Series, winning three of them. Ask him to pick a favorite Series, and he talks in circles. So, pick out one yourself and sit back and listen to what Sparky has to say. Let's try the 1975 World Series, the one in which the Reds won in seven, but only after Boston's Carlton Fisk had dramatically won the sixth game for the Bosox with a home run off the left-field foul pole. Anderson:*

Boston is one of those special places in which to play baseball. Once you've been there—and I had never been there until 1975—you find that this is a city that cares more about its baseball team than does any other city in the United

States. We had a few rainouts, and that gave me some time to go around the city and experience this place and its people. Boston really does love their Red Sox.

The thing I never forget about Boston Red Sox fans is that if the opposing team makes a great play, they will give them a hand. You won't consistently see that in any other place but Boston. It is an amazing thing.

After Game Six was over (on Fisk's twelfth-inning homer), I was sick about the whole thing, losing a game like that. To get to our team bus, we had to walk all the way under the stands from the third-base side around to right field. I was feeling really down as we walked along. All of a sudden someone walks up behind me, puts his hand on my shoulder, and says, "Skip, wasn't that the greatest game you've ever played in?"

It was Pete. I looked at him and said, "You know, Peter, let me tell you something: You're nuts. I'm not going to sleep tonight, and you're telling me that this was the greatest game you've ever been involved in?"

Then he said, "Well, yeah, because we're going to top the whole thing off by winning tomorrow." And Tony Perez adds, "Don't worry, Skeep, we're going to beat them tomorrow."

Oh, these guys weren't perfect; there was nothing goody-goody about them. But you can't get much closer to perfection than they were.

<hr/>

BILL LEE, *then a pitcher with the Red Sox, offers a unique Spaceman spin on that 1975 World Series:*

Think of it as a mathematical equation. You'd have Red Sox and Red Machine, and the "Red" cancels out, leaving you with Sox Machine. Bring on James Brown.

The Reds were really good, but I'm telling you, their pitching staff wasn't that dominant. Gullet didn't have a good Series, and I came within one pitch of winning Game Two and one pitch from winning Game Seven. If things had been different, and if the (Ed) Armbrister call had been different, and if we turn the double play on the Bench grounder in Game Seven, and I don't throw the hanging curveball to (Tony) Perez, and I don't start the ninth inning of Game Two . . . We were as good as they were, and it was a classic Series for all the what-ifs.

Rose was the heart and soul of that ballclub. He was like the starter, the hustling guy who got everyone else going. Then you had Joe Morgan, who was graceful and a good hitter. You go right down the line, and they could hit all the way through their lineup. They didn't have an easy out in that lineup, and that's why they were so dominant.

You've also got to remember that for that whole '75 Series, we were without our number-two player, Jim Rice.

Sports Illustrated's RON FIMRITE wrote this about Rose when he was named SI's Sportsman of the Year, referring to the seventh game of 1975 World Series in which the Reds beat Boston, 4–3:

The sheer force of his personality was felt more compellingly in the sixth inning of the final game. The Reds had closed an early 3–0 Red Sox lead to 3–2 on Perez's home run. . . . There was someone on base for Perez to drive home only because Rose, sliding with typical fury into second, had intimidated Denny Doyle into throwing wildly to first on what would have been an inning-ending double play. Now, with the Red Sox about to come to bat, Rose gave an astonishing performance. He set about rousing his teammates, as if they were troops on the front line. He bellowed encouragement, pounded his fist into his glove, and bounced about the infield with an enthusiasm that was contagious. He

PHOTO COURTESY OF CINCINNATI REDS

Rose takes a throw at third against the Boston Red Sox in the 1975 World Series.

seemed to grow physically in stature, to tower over the situation. Even in the stands his will to win could be felt. Though they still trailed in the game, it seemed inevitable the Reds would win. It was a highly charged moment of a kind rarely, if ever, seen in a major-league baseball game. Rose had stirred his teammates, hardened professionals, to a collegiate pitch.[2]

Over the years, although exact opposites in many respects, Rose and Bill Lee became pretty good friends. **LEE:**

Pete's tough, one of those guys who would run through hell in a gasoline suit. He's the one guy other players hated the most, but if you were going to draft a ballclub, he's the one guy you would start your ballclub off with because of his tenacity.

I remember playing against him, first of all, in the 1975 World Series when I was with the Red Sox. He was Most Valuable Player in that Series. He was instrumental in the seventh game, when he was on first and ran to second on a ground ball that Johnny Bench hit. Pete ran into second base in such a way that it forced our second baseman, Denny Doyle, to throw wildly to first while avoiding being taken out by Pete. Then Perez hit a home run, next batter up. That's the kind of guy Rose was—played hard and hustled all the time.

At the end of the Series, I had to go to New York and present him with the Most Valuable Player Award, which was an AMC Pacer. I thought that was great because it was such a little horsesh— car. He ended up driving it across the street to another dealership and trading it in as a down payment on a Rolls Royce. He kind of got the final word on that one. I was the one picked to present him with the award because they wanted an opposing player to do it, and I guess they thought I was a pretty talkative guy. Most of the other guys on the Red Sox were reluctant to do it. I did it kind of reluctantly, but then I figured that the Pacer was kind of a punishment for him, so I kind of took a liking to it.

The funny thing is that when Pete bought the Rolls Royce, it was registered in his wife Karolyn's name. Then they got divorced. Pete kept the Rolls and ended up giving it to his girlfriend. Sometime later, Karolyn had the girlfriend pulled over and made a citizen's arrest, saying that the car had been put in her name and was therefore stolen. That got Pete's new girlfriend locked up, although I don't remember which one of Pete's girlfriends that was. Karolyn's the one who told me this story, and I thought it was a hoot. I never did get to ride in that Rolls, although I once rode in an old burgundy one that (former Boston Bruins player) Derek Sanderson had.

BUD HARRELSON would go on to become manager of the Mets for two seasons, 1990 and 1991, just missing the chance to manage against his old nemesis, Rose. Harrelson looks back one more time on the Big Red Machine and then Rose as skipper:

The Big Red Machine was the type of team that you could just sit back and watch. That's not the team that Pete had while he was managing the Reds. He moved guys, ran guys, hit-and-run. It was action baseball. I guarantee you that the one thing he expected, like I did, was that guys give it their all for nine innings or however many innings it took, then worry about the next day the next day. It would have been fun managing against him, and I'm just sorry I never got that chance.

⬧

Bob Howsam:

When I think of the Big Red Machine, I think of a balanced ballclub that could do everything in every area. Excellent defense, good arms, and power and speed on offense. And I think our pitching was a lot better than people gave us credit for.

In 1976 we swept the Phillies in the league series, then went on to beat the Yankees in four straight to win the World Series. You don't do that without people who can throw the ball and do a good job.

⬧

Rose's last hurrah with the Big Red Machine was his forty-four-game hitting streak in 1978, his final season with the Reds before signing with the Phillies as a free agent. A nation watched as Rose, then thirty-seven years old, chased another record, one belonging to one of his idols, Joe DiMaggio. Atlanta relief pitcher **Gene Garber** *stopped Rose's streak at forty-four, getting him to line into a double play in the seventh inning and then striking him out in the ninth as the Braves won, 16–4. Garber:*

There was one thing on my mind and that was to throw strikes. The last thing in the world I wanted to do was walk him and have the streak come to an end that way. I mean, I wanted the streak to go on. It's been a fantastic contribution

to interest in baseball. But I wanted to get him out. That's
what I'm paid to do.[3]

PETE ROSE, *on Garber's stopping his hitting streak:*

People still ask me for my exact thoughts when the streak
ended, when I struck out. And the answer is, I don't remember anymore. I know I wasn't thinking, *Good going, Garber.*
My exact thoughts? They're coming back. I was angry. That
was my exact thought. Anger. Not *Lay the ball down the middle, Garber. Hit the corners. Do what you want. But fight me
man to man. Don't walk me.*[4]

4

PHIL 'ER UP

Diehard Reds fans took a double hit in the gut after the 1978 season. Sparky Anderson was fired after the team posted a second-place finish with a 92–69 record, and Pete Rose left via free agency, eventually to sign with the Philadelphia Phillies.

Nineteen seventy-eight had been a vintage year for Rose: the then-National League-record forty-four-game hitting streak; a league-leading fifty-one doubles; a .302 batting average, 103 runs scored, and even thirteen steals, his third-highest single-season total. Still, Reds officials had put the word out that they thought Rose's bat and basepath speed were slowing. At age thirty-seven, Rose supposedly was winding down. Maybe it was time to cut the umbilical cord.

By this time, Bob Howsam also had left the Reds, opting for early retirement because of a bad back. Howsam's replacement, Dick Wagner, didn't seem too keen about keeping Rose around. On October 1, the Reds claimed in a press release that they had offered Rose a deal that would make him the highest-paid player in club history. Reuven Katz, Rose's attorney, calmly disputed the claim, saying that by his calculations, the Reds' offer would make Rose only the second- or third-highest-paid player on the current Reds teams.

Rose was wooed by a number of clubs, finally settling on the Phils, whose offer was heavier on World Series-ring potential than it was money. Philadelphia was coming off three consecutive National League East titles, although they failed to make it to the World Series those years. In Rose's second season with the Phils, they beat Kansas City to win the 1980 World Series, and returned to the Series in 1983, only to lose in five games to the Baltimore Orioles, the same franchise that had beaten the Reds in 1970, the year Rose made his first World Series appearance.

DAVE BRISTOL probably knows Rose as well as any of Pete's other former managers do, or did. He saw Rose's move to the Phillies as a win-win situation:

Pete Rose is what the Phillies needed, and that's why they got him over there. He was the difference in them being so good in 1980. Pete is the one that got them over the hump and taught them how to win.

BILL CONLIN, a sportswriter for the Philadelphia Daily News since 1965, covered the Phillies from 1966 though 1987 and has been a columnist since then. He was there when Rose came to Philadelphia, and recalls the scenario leading up to Rose's ballyhooed signing:

Pete wanted to come to Philadelphia, and the Phils were the first stop on his "grand tour." But when Bob and Ruly Carpenter found out what it was going to cost them over five years, they balked and thanked Pete very much.

When Pete's attorney, Reuven Katz, ran a dollar figure past them, it was less than what other teams, such as the Atlanta Braves, had been offering, about $1 million a year. The Phils said, "Sorry, that's too rich for our blood," and then team President William Giles drove Rose and Katz to the airport.

Katz and Rose had flown in on a chartered plane, and they asked the Phils if they would foot the bill for the charter. Ruly told them that they were on their own, but that he would have Giles drive them to the airport. On the way there, Giles told them, "Don't give up on us. I'll see what I can work out."

Atlanta, Saint Louis, Kansas City, and Pittsburgh were the main stops for Pete's tour. All of them had substantial and creative offers for Pete. Where (Braves owner Ted) Turner was offering the $1 million a year, Ewing Kauffman in Kansas City was offering less money but some stock in a pharmaceutical company. Gussie Busch also offered less money, but with an Anheuser-Busch distributorship to be his once his playing days were over, just as he had done with Roger Maris. That's a nice golden parachute.

The most intriguing offer might have come from John Galbreath of the Pirates. He's the only guy in history with both a World Series trophy and a Kentucky Derby trophy in his trophy case. The deal was not nearly as much money as Turner was offering, but with the money would come the service of a brood mare and X number of shots from Kentucky Derby-winning studs. When Pete heard that, his legs turned to jelly because he had a fondness not only for betting but also for horses.

These were all great deals, but the one trump card the Phillies still had was that Pete was already good friends with their top players, such as Mike Schmidt, Greg Luzinski, and Garry Maddox. He admired the way the ballclub had been put together. It reminded him of the early days of the Big Red Machine, looking very much like a team about to break through.

Pete and Reuven made it very clear that they would accept a little less money. So Giles went to Channel 17, which held the team's broadcast rights, and asked them to consider renegotiating their contract to provide the extra money the team needed to sign Pete. Giles promised station officials that their ratings and ad revenue would go way up with Pete Rose on board. As it turns out, the increased cash flow turned out to be about threefold what the Phils had projected in laying out their offer to Pete.

WILLIAM GILES, *the Phillies' team president, was instrumental in bringing Pete Rose to Philadelphia:*

His signing was the most exciting and dramatically effective thing that we've ever done here. Within two months after we'd announced that we signed him, we sold $2.5 million more in season tickets than we'd ever sold before. So in two months we made back almost three times the money that we'd signed him for.

What Pete said at the time, and I agreed with him, was that there were really only two people in the game who put extra people in the stands—himself and Dave Parker. This was in the late seventies, and in my judgment, Pete put a lot more people in the seats than Parker.[1]

BILL CONLIN *discusses how the Rose acquisition affected the team's chemistry:*

The Phils thought he would be able to do one thing: take a lot of the pressure off sensitive guys like Mike Schmidt. Now when the press came barging through the doors, they would go straight to Pete's locker, and that lightened the load on Schmidt et al. considerably. By then, (Steve) Carlton wasn't speaking to the media at all, and Luzinski's knees were starting to break down.

This is a team that had long been a very cranky, anti-media club, and Rose was a tremendous breath of fresh air at a time when we, the press, were straining to find something fresh to write about a club that had won three straight divisional titles without making it to the World Series.

By the time Rose got to the Phillies, slugger **GREG LUZINSKi**, *who had originally signed with Philadelphia in 1968, had become something of a fan favorite, a second fiddle to Mike Schmidt in the Phillies' power-hitting structure. Luzinski:*

Pete had been a great player with the Reds, and we had played Cincinnati in the playoffs when he was a part of the Big Red Machine. We were a younger club at that time, and they had a seasoned club.

Free agency was still a fairly new thing at that time, and to get a player of Pete's caliber who could plug into the lead-off spot was big for us. There was no problem in terms of team chemistry. We had some guys already on the club, forming the nucleus, who had come up together within a year or two of each other. Our general manager, Paul Owens, had a pretty good feel for bringing people in to help get us over the hump so we could get to the World Series. There's no question Rose was a part of that. We fell short in '75 without him and then won it with him in '80.

There's no question players looked up to him. Pete had a knack for being able to say things and then go out and back it up out on the field. He might say, "I'm going to get two or three hits tonight," and he'd get them.

The unique thing about Rose's coming to Philadelphia is that Bowa, Schmitty, and myself already knew Pete pretty well. We had on occasion talked to him around the batting cage, and we knew him as a guy who would do anything to win a game. Paul Owens already knew how we felt about Pete before he went out to sign him, so there really was no need for him to come to us and ask us what we thought about it.

It is generally known that Rose played a key role in getting Schmidt to ratchet up his game, pushing a good player to become a Hall of Fame candidate. **LUZINSKI:**

Pete was a big influence on Mike Schmidt, and they ended up having a real close rapport. There's no question that Pete helped Schmitty develop his career. Pete had a way of making Mike feel comfortable, and Mike certainly had the ability to be a truly great player. Not that Pete did it for him— Mike had to go out and do it himself.

A lot of it had to do with the confidence factor. Pete and Mike loved to talk baseball together, and Pete would talk to Mike about his (Schmidt's) abilities. It rubbed off. I'm sure Pete tried to do that with other players, but there's a difference from player to player in how they accept that. Mike listened closely to Pete and took it to heart.

There are different kinds of leaders. There are leaders in the clubhouse and leaders on the field. Pete played the game hard, obviously, and not only was it an inspiration to watch him play, but it was actually enjoyable. But he also wasn't afraid to step on people's egos and tell them when they weren't carrying their weight.

◄○►

Schmidt wasn't the only Phillies player who benefited from some of Rose rubbing off on him. DICKIE NOLES pitched for Philadelphia during three of the years, 1979–81, that Rose was there:

I was in the minor leagues at the start of the 1979 season and got called up July 4. I had grown up a Cincinnati Reds fan, as well as a Braves fan. But it was hard not to like the Big Red Machine. I'm from North Carolina, and with Tommy Helms being from North Carolina, we pulled for Tommy and, along with him, the Reds. To me, the Big Red Machine started in 1970, although most people associate it with 1975.

Pete Rose was the kind of ballplayer that any young kid in the 1970s would have been infatuated with. He ran to first base, got two hundred hits, and played on a great team. His hustle turned everyone on to him. He was a great player.

So when he joined the Phillies, to me, it was like, "Oh, my goodness!" There were a few other big names playing at the time—Mike Schmidt, Reggie Jackson, Nolan Ryan—but none of them were as big as Pete Rose. Jackson came the closest because he had that same kind of persona about him. But Rose was the top dog.

The thing I remember most about Pete was his compassion toward teammates. He had a way of making you feel good. I had been on the club just long enough to pitch one game, and here was Pete talking to me like someone who really cared about me. He was like that with everybody. If you were doing something wrong, he would come over and tell you how to do it. If you were struggling with something, he would be there to help. I think a lot of people miss that about him.

I've heard things about Pete that aren't so good, such as his being motivated by his own success. Well, what great player isn't? The great thing about Pete was that once he met you and heard your name, he would never forget it. He had a great memory, and he treated me like gold. He even kind of looked after me and gave me a nickname, for cryin' out loud—"Pieface." When Pete Rose gives you a nickname, whether you like it or not, you take it. I'm forty-six years old and still can't get rid of it.

BUD HARRELSON, *Rose's former fight foe, allied himself with Rose when he joined the Phils for part of the 1979 season. By then, much had been forgiven. Harrelson:*

Pete was not very vocal, only when he had to be. They already had Mike Schmidt, Greg Luzinski, and Lefty (Steve Carlton) there, some guys who had already had pretty strong careers. But they certainly weren't Pete Rose.

I had nothing but respect for Pete, even though we had had our differences in 1973. Even in 1977, when Tom Seaver had gotten traded over to the Reds by the Mets, Pete told him, "That little SOB (Harrelson) didn't know me well enough to call me those names." But we got along. In 1974 I once hit a home run over his head in left field. Coming off the field, he waited near shortstop long enough to say to me, "What the hell was all that about?" I said, "I don't know."

Pete just went about his business. He was all-pro. He just did his job and didn't complain about one thing. A lot of guys complain. Not Pete. He didn't complain about the managers, the owners, the conditions, whatever. He loved the game.

HARRELSON, *on Mike Schmidt, before Rose came to Philadelphia:*

I was playing second and short in 1978, and I can remember Mike Schmidt sitting down next to me and being frustrated.

He would say, "What the hell am I doing, Bud?" I turn around and say, "You're asking me? Hey, there's the batting instructor over there. I'm not going to say anything, Mike. . . . Keep swinging."

We look at Hall of Fame guys and think of them as supermen. They're not; they're just men. They're just guys, and they can get up and down. Rose seemed to be as consistent as anybody, just playing through distractions or playing hurt. The guy was amazing, and that had to rub off on the other guy.

BILL CONLIN:

Pete played very well that first year with the Phils. He started his stretch run toward a possible batting title by going 5–for–5 in New York, which was on the same day that Karolyn filed for divorce.

I remember that day quite clearly. I was leaving my hotel to go to the ballpark and got onto the same elevator with John Vukovich. It stopped about two floors down, and on stepped Pete, and we could see that he was really steaming. Usually, he would be real friendly and start chatting with us, but not this time.

Vuckovich says to Pete, "You look really ticked off, Pete. What's up?"

"She filed."

We knew there had long been trouble in the marriage, but now it was official, and we caught him just after he had found out how much money this was going to cost him. A lot, and with it would go all the public allegations of his infidelities. He said, "There's only one thing to do tonight, and that's to get five knocks." And that's exactly what he did.

Pete proceeded to get more hits in September than anyone else in the National League and came within a whisker of winning the batting title.

━☉━

*By 1979 there was little about Pete Rose that most in and around the game had not discovered, but **DICKIE NOLES** was surprised by one facet of Rose once they became Phillies teammates midway through the 1979 season:*

His talent surprised me. Everybody says Pete wasn't the most talented person out there, that he had all this desire and dedication but little talent. Well, when this guy got into the batter's box and hit the baseball, you could see he was a very talented man. He had to have a talent for hitting the baseball—he did get more hits than anyone else in the history of the game. And the way he ran bases and his professionalism on the field . . . they don't get much better than that.

If he made errors, they weren't dumb errors. They were errors that every human being makes. And hitting? He hit the ball hard.

One of the things I got out of watching him—and this was after he got two hundred hits and hit over .300 at age thirty-nine—was how impressive he was while playing at an age when most other guys had retired. His age didn't show on the field.

━☉━

***DICKIE NOLES**, on the Phils before and after Rose joined the ballclub:*

If you have played with Pete, you don't have to have seen what the team was like before to know that he was making a difference. His impact on a team is tremendous. He's energetic, he's enthusiastic, and he doesn't take losing really well. His will to win is incredible. Defeat for him is agony. He's ready to go every day to figure out a way to win. That becomes contagious.

-=◊=-

BILL CONLIN *was among many journalists over the years who were charmed by Rose's media savvy and accessibility, but he also knew that Rose wasn't beloved by all his teammates in Philadelphia. Conlin:*

Some guys resented him, seeing him as this big shot coming in and taking over the club. One of those guys was pitcher Ron Reed, the six-foot-six former basketball player who was an anti-media guy anyway. He resented the hell out of Pete's being there.

Reed and Rose had a near-fistfight one time on a charter flight between Oklahoma City and Houston. The Phillies had been at Oklahoma City that day to play their top farm club, and it had been a long day, with a thunderstorm delaying the departure out of Oklahoma City.

I was on that flight, and it was obvious that everyone was tired and in a sour mood. On top of that, Pete and Ron rarely spoke to each other anyway. Reed, being a really big guy, was trying to stretch out in his seat to get some rest and had his knees squinched up against the back of the seat in front of him. Well, Pete happened to be in that seat in front of Reed, and Pete was trying to sleep. That's usually what he did on planes, because he wasn't one to play cards on the plane with the other guys.

At one point, Pete tried to push his seat back, and it sort of sprang back on Reed's knees, hitting them. That's when Reed took a foot and violently kicked the back of Pete's seat, almost knocking Pete forward out of his seat. Pete jumped up and went back to get Ron, and they started going at it. Danny Ozark, the manager, himself an enormous guy at six-foot-five, got in between them and pried them apart.

Pete and Ron eventually shook hands, and that was that. Pete wasn't universally loved, but he was universally

respected. He filled his role well as a catalyst to that team, and
he was a spotlight magnet, and that's what that team needed.

⊏◯⊐

*Prior to Rose's arrival in Philadelphia, the Phillies hadn't
won a World Series since 1950. That dry spell ended
in 1980, when Rose batted . 282 and helped the Phils
to a world championship by knocking off the George
Brett-led Kansas City Royals. The Phils that year were a
classic example of a team that was better than the
sum of its parts, with only one starter hitting over .300
(Bake McBride at .309), one player with at least
twenty home runs (Schmidt, with forty-eight), and just
two pitchers with more than seven victories (Steve
Carlton, with twenty-four, and Dick Ruthven, with
seventeen). Veteran baseball writer TRACY RINGOLSBY
remembers that Series, however, as something other
than Rose's finest moment:*

I remember how he had the tantrum when he wasn't in the
lineup. That bugged me, because he was supposed to be the
ultimate team guy. That was another side of Pete right there,
the selfishness. That kind of soured me on him.

⊏◯⊐

GREG LUZINSKI:

Even as late as it was in his career when he came to us, Pete
would take batting practice on days off. He didn't take a lot, but
baseball was his life and he would always be swinging at bat.
Everything he did was centered around the game of baseball.

Pete received a lot of credit for what he did with us, and
rightfully so. He was pretty much the catalyst of our club.

It's a shame that he's not in the Hall of Fame. Statistically,
he belongs there. I have no idea of the circumstances behind

his being banned from baseball—that's between him and the commissioner's office.

BUD HARRELSON *offers further evidence of Rose's leadership savvy:*

One time we got rained out of a game and were making plans to reschedule it for later in the season, probably as part of a doubleheader. But Ruly Carpenter came to us and asked us to give up an off-day so that we could use that day to make up the game.

I kept my mouth shut because I was kind of the new guy. The players took a vote and voted it down, choosing not to play. Pete stood up in the middle of the room and said, "Listen, when you ask for something, does Ruly Carpenter give it to you?"

"Yeahhhh."

"Well, Ruly's asking for you to play on an off-day. Did you guys come here to play baseball or what? I think you ought to re-vote."

We did and it was pretty much unanimous—we re-voted to play. At least, no one objected to what he was saying. But you have to get both teams to vote, and whoever it was we were supposed to play voted it down. Ruly Carpenter, in his mind, got a plus vote from his players.

DICKIE NOLES *gives another example of Rose's influence on the Phillies:*

Pete made them all better, every one of them. He did it by the way he played on the field and by getting into their heads in a positive way.

One time we were down 5–2 to Nolan Ryan and the Houston Astros. I mean, this was the fifth game of the

National League playoff series, and God was out there pitching against us. The energy that Pete then put into the guys on the bench was incredible. At one point you could see the heads on our players starting to droop, and that's when Pete turned to Larry Bowa, who was getting ready to bat, and said, "Hey, Bowa, if you get on here, we'll turn this thing around and win this game." Pete just believed it and he knew it, and this fired us up.

Bowa got on, and Pete proceeded to put his money where his mouth was by working the count to eventually get a walk with the bases loaded. This was a guy who could turn a game around with a walk.

*In one sense, the Rose-Harrelson rivalry still simmered when both men got to the Phils. A grinning **BUD HARRELSON** explains how:*

Pete Rose Jr. and my son Tim are about the same age, maybe just a few months apart. They spent a lot of time together at the ballpark, and the Phils were really good about that, letting our kids hang around.

Out on the field, while we were taking batting practice, there was a place where kids could shoot baskets and entertain themselves. All of a sudden, during a break, one of the batboys runs out and says, "Rose and Harrelson are fighting in the batting cage!" And there they were—Pete and Tim, who were about nine or ten at the time, were going at it. Pete and I immediately turned around to the batboy and said, "Who's winning? Who's winning?"

*Bill **Conlin** offers another perspective on a key moment in the 1980 World Series:*

Pete had a solid 1980 but nothing spectacular. He couldn't lead off much anymore, but the Phils were fortunate to have Bake McBride to step in there.

As far as playing first base, Pete was an intelligent defensive player who never hurt them in the field, although one of the most memorable plays he ever made was actually a screw-up. That's the catch he made in Game Six of the World Series, when he caught a foul pop that bounced off catcher Bob Boone's glove.

That should have been Pete's ball in the first place. It was well down the line, drifting toward the stands, and Pete got a late break on the ball. Fortunately for Pete, Boone was hustling all the way from home plate, about seventy feet away, to get under the ball as best he could, even though he was in no position to get a good look at it. The ball glanced off of Boone's glove, and Pete lunged and got his glove under the ball to look like the hero, when in fact he should have been the goat.

5

HOME AGAIN

I n the last year, 1983, of his five-year contract with the Phillies, Rose batted .245. The team didn't renew the contract, and so Rose was cut loose to find another deal elsewhere.

At the age of forty-two, soon to be forty-three, Rose still had work to do. By the end of 1983, he had closed to within 201 of Ty Cobb's career hits record, with 3,990, and he needed someplace to go in order to keep the at-bats coming. Even if it meant heading north to Canada.

On Friday, January 20, 1984, Rose signed a one-year contract with the Montreal Expos, a team headed nowhere despite the additional talents of Gary Carter, Andre Dawson, and Tim Raines.

PHOTO COURTESY OF MONTREAL EXPOS

When the Phillies wouldn't re-sign Rose after the 1983 season, he went north to the Montreal Expos. Here he's pictured with Expos President John McHale.

Meanwhile, back in Cincy, groundwork was being laid that would eventually bring Rose back to the Reds. Bob Howsam had returned on a long-term temporary basis to help the ownership team of Bill and Jim Williams perform a badly needed makeover of the Reds. Also back in the saddle was Tony Perez, who also had played for the Phils in 1983.

The move back to Cincinnati rejuvenated Rose. He was hitting .259 in a reserve role with the Expos, but he batted .365 over the last six weeks of the season with the Reds.

Longtime Cincinnati Enquirer *sportswriter and columnist* **TIM SULLIVAN,** *who had covered the downtrodden Rose-less Reds in the early eighties as a beat writer, found his interest in the Reds piqued when word came that Rose would be returning to Cincinnati. Sullivan:*

What I remember about his return to Cincinnati was the level of excitement that the story created. In my mind, the night that he returned was as exciting and gripping, maybe even more so, than the night he broke Ty Cobb's hits record. The circumstances under which he had left Cincinnati had never settled right with the people of the city, who had wanted to see him back.

In the fall of 1983 I had come out with the story that Tony Perez would be coming back to Cincinnati, and to many people the fact that Perez was returning to the Reds meant that Rose would not be. The Reds had (again) changed general managers, and the guy who had let Pete Rose go, Dick Wagner, was no longer in charge. Bob Howsam, who ultimately brought Pete back, recognized the P.R. value of bringing back at least part of the Big Red Machine. When he brought Perez back, I think Pete's reaction was that "I'm probably not going to be able to come home."

If memory serves me right, Milton Richmond of United Press International is the one who broke the story that Pete would be returning. I was working the desk that night, and the guy who was covering the team for us at the time was Greg Hoard. Greg had been working on a story from the standpoint of Vern Rapp losing his job (as manager of the Reds), and the other side of the story was that Pete was coming home. So we reworked that story that night to work in all of what was happening, and I think the headline was "Pete Comes Home," and you didn't have to explain to anybody who "Pete" was.

Then, that first night back, when he came to the plate and hit that line drive that skipped through for a base hit— it might have either been a single and a two-base error or a double and just an error—and Pete came diving headfirst into third base, the place just went wild. Everything that happened with the hit record was kind of anticlimactic, because you knew he was going to get it anyway.

ROSE, *on his return to Cincinnati:*

There aren't many things I back away from. If they wouldn't let me play back home in Cincinnati, then I was damned if I was going to manage. I'd hang in at Montreal and take my chances, as a free agent it looked like, the following year. But I *wanted* to come home and be with the Reds when they won a pennant. I wanted to come home, like a kid who forgot his school lunch somewhere and is standing in the yard smelling his mother's cooking through a window. No. More than that. I wanted to come home more than that. Forty-three or not, I *knew* I could still hit. I wasn't ready to stop. I wouldn't stop. But who wanted me? A tight time. Cobb? I knew every hit Cobb had and every hit I had. I may not be a college graduate—I ain't— but I can count.[1]

SHELDON "CHIEF" BENDER, *the Reds' longtime player personnel director, offers these thoughts on bringing Rose back to the Reds:*

We talked about the condition of the franchise, and the more we talked, the more it made sense to bring Pete back. We needed something to get people excited again. (Bob) Howsam felt he should come back just as manager, and then later when Pete said he wanted to play, Howsam insisted that he be called a manager-player instead of a player-manager, although that phrase never took.

We felt Pete was over the hill and couldn't help the club that much. But damned if he didn't bounce back again and get some hits. But Howsam didn't want him to play as much as he did. I guess you could say Pete misled him on how much he was going to put himself in the lineup.

He ended up hurting the careers of a couple of our younger guys—Paul O'Neill, Kal Daniels, mostly Nick Esasky. Their playing time depended some on if the manager played, and that's a tough spot for a young guy. It wasn't fair. He cost Esasky a couple years of his career.[2]

*When **BOB HOWSAM** returned to the Reds in 1983, after retiring in 1978 with a bad back, he did it with the idea that it would be on an interim/consulting basis. Howsam:*

I brought Pete back to manage for us. I talked to Pete hour after hour to find out for myself if I thought he could come back and be a manager. I finally decided he could, so we brought him back, and he was extremely popular.

As it turned out, Rose never was the manager that I thought he would be. What held him back was that he wouldn't listen to people who could help him, like George Sherger, who I put on the bench with Rose. George knew how to run a ballgame as well as anybody I've ever known. He was the first guy that Sparky Anderson had wanted to bring with him to Cincinnati in 1970 to be a coach, because he had played for him.

You have to listen to people who can help you so as to shorten the amount of time you need to become good at something. Pete wouldn't do it, I'm sorry to say.

HOWSAM *continues:*

The P.R. aspect was part of the reason for bringing Pete back to the Reds. Before we brought him back, I would sit in the stands, and it had gotten to where all our fans were sitting on their hands most of the time. That's what it had come to.

That's why I asked my oldest son, Robert Jr., who was in advertising in New York, to come to Cincinnati on weekends to run some surveys for me. We talked to many fans as part of our research, and out of that we came up with the slogan

"Having Fun Again." Our attendance started coming back up, and we started having fun again.

⌁

*Friend and former teammate **TOMMY HELMS** was reunited with Rose when Pete asked him to stay on as a coach with the Reds:*

I was already here coaching when he came back. I thought he did a heckuva job managing—I thought he could have won manager of the year there in 1985, when we came back and finished second. There were times I thought he was more into the game as a player-manager than as just a non-playing manager.

We finished second four years in a row, but we just couldn't get it over the hump. He was a players' manager. He wanted you to hustle your butt every day. "Gimme all you got, and if you don't want to, go somewhere else or something."

He was a great guy to work for because he delegated well and trusted his coaches to do what was right.

⌁

*Rose always made it a point to keep track of who the beat writers were covering the Reds, even when he was no longer playing for the team. **TIM SULLIVAN:***

I hadn't dealt with him much prior to 1984. But I do remember being in Philadelphia once while covering the Reds at the time, and Pete was holding court with reporters. I was still new on the beat—this must have been 1981—but he looked over at me and said, "You must be Tim Sullivan."

For the next thirty or forty minutes he had my attention, telling all kinds of stories and jokes and talking about this and that. I was pretty young then and spellbound by it. I ended up writing this sort of rapturous column about what an irresistible character he was.

He knew that his hometown paper had a new guy on the beat. He was certainly attendant to all those kinds of things. I remember the first time I ever talked to him was over the phone,

PHOTO COURTESY OF CINCINNATI REDS

Back home in Cincinnati, player-manager Pete Rose connects on another of his more than 4,000 hits.

when I took a call that was meant for our baseball writer, Bob Hertzel. It was on deadline, and he had just signed a new contract—this would have been in either 1977 or 1978.

He said, "Is Hertzel there?"

I said, "Well, he's on deadline."

"This is Pete Rose."

"Oh, hold the line. I'll get him for you."

SULLIVAN *got better acquainted with Rose after Rose returned to the Reds, first as player-manager, then as just manager.*

Pete had pluses and minuses as a manager. There were some guys who responded to him pretty well, but I don't know that his heart was ever completely in it.

In spring training, he would rarely go on road trips, which is pretty unusual for a manager. I remember going to

Vero Beach (Florida), which is a real grind to get to from Plant City. You had to drive across the state, and you had all these little roads. Driving back at night, it can be a little dangerous. You go through a place called Yeehaw Junction, a little two-lane road that is very dark. If you have any car trouble, there's really no place to stop for miles and miles.

When I got to Vero, Tommy Lasorda came up and said, "Where's Pete?" It was explained to him that Pete wasn't on the trip, that he had stayed back at the complex.

This sort of thing persisted. Frequently when the Reds were on the road, Pete would drive his car—he wouldn't take the bus with the rest of the team. I thought that set a bad example. Plus he had a conflict of interest with himself as a player, and players were all supposed to be on the team bus together. I think it was Joe Torre who said, "Pete will become a manager the day he pinch hits for himself."

DAVE BRISTOL, *who rejoined Rose as a Reds coach in the late eighties, gives his own assessment of Rose's managing skills:*

Well, first of all, he finished second (in the National League West) about every year while he was managing. People say you needed to win to prove yourself, but I thought he did pretty well with what he had. It's just a shame that he got in trouble, because otherwise we'd all probably still be there— Pete, me, Tommy Helms, and Perez. I don't think Marge Schott ever would have fired him.

Tommy Helms was the bench coach, and Pete listened an awful lot to Tommy. If Pete liked what Tommy said, he'd do it. If not, he wouldn't do it. Pete used his coaches very well.

The thing that surprised me most of all was the fact that more of his players didn't go to him for help with their hitting. He wasn't one who would force himself on anybody, but he was always there early and very approachable. Some of those guys really needed help, and here's a guy who's one of the greatest hitters in the history of the game. Some took advantage of it, but many didn't. . . . I just don't know. God, Pete would've helped anybody.

✦

*Longtime baseball man **GLENN SAMPLE**, already quite familiar with Rose as player, got to know him as a manager. For many years, Sample has worked as official scorer at Reds home games, including the years that Rose was managing there. Sample:*

I never got a complaint from Pete Rose once on any call or scoring decision. The way they work it at Cincinnati is that I would never get a direct call from a player complaining about one of my scoring calls. They were to relay word to the public relations manager if they wanted me to review the play, and this was back before they had instant replay in the official scorer's booth. An official scorer had twenty-four hours to review and change a call.

After the game I would go over to the scoreboard room from where they ran the scoreboard. They also had it set up to where you could watch replays, and I'd go in there to review a disputed decision. A couple of times I remember going in there between innings instead of after the game, running three booths down to review this and then running back before the next half-inning started—all in about two minutes.

Some of the Reds players would call, but I never got one from Pete himself.

I thought he was a pretty good manager. When he first got there, the Reds were really struggling. They had lost a hundred and some games the year before he returned. Just when he left, they were ready to do something. (Lou) Piniella came in the next year, and they won the World

Series. Pete had something to do with that. Pete had brought up a lot of those kids from the minors and helped get them to the brink of success.

⋅◁▷⋅

*Not all of the Reds players bought into Rose's managerial shtick. Take **NICK ESASKY**, for instance. It was Esasky who was hurt most by Rose's stint as player-manager, for it was Esasky's first-base position that Rose usually used when inserting himself into the lineup in 1984–86. Esasky:*

After a while Pete didn't try to hide the fact that he didn't like me. He would say things to reporters like, "He's too easygoing, I don't know if he cares, I don't know how much Nick really wants it." You know, all that stuff. But I cared plenty. I just didn't show it in the same way a Peter Rose does. Everybody's got their own style. What it came down to was, anytime I was playing first base, Pete wanted to be there instead.[1]

⋅◁▷⋅

***TIM SULLIVAN** offers some additional insights on Rose as manager:*

I think he still was cutting some corners on things he could have done. He continued to not make road trips in spring training, even after he had stopped playing. Or he might show up at the last minute, driving there with the pitching coach or whatever.

In retrospect, you look back and have to wonder what he was doing with his time. Why was he so busy? And it makes you think that maybe the gambling had started earlier than we had perceived.

━☼━

DAVE BRISTOL saw things a bit differently, such as during the tense times in 1989 in the midst of Major League Baseball's investigation of Rose's alleged gambling habits:

Pitching coach Scott Reed and I were in the car with Pete going to Saint Petersburg when that story broke about his alleged involvement in gambling. As soon as we got to the ballpark and got out of the car, we were greeted by hordes of reporters. Every day this went on, and every day Pete handled the media perfectly. He answered all their questions. But when the game started, it was all managing and running the team, and he never let this other stuff affect him one iota.

There is a certain kind of genius that it takes to be able to focus like that with all this other stuff going on around you. That's how he was able to get over four thousand hits. When the game started, he was ready to play. Nothing got in his way, especially when it came to getting a base hit. Pete has a pretty thick skin, although when you ever get around to putting the needle in him, he can come back at you pretty quickly.

6

CHASING TY COBB

Well into his forties, Charlie Hustle needed a carrot. His days as a valued Reds superstar were long past, the Phillies had given up on him, and the Montreal Expos were basically tolerating him. By mid-1984, Rose the player was slowing down, winding down, and counting down toward Ty Cobb's career hits record of 4,191. That was the carrot, a lifetime-achievement statistical award that had once been considered unattainable.

America's fascination with statistical landmarks was exceeded in intensity only by Rose's. He was a numbers nut with a head for statistics and the baseball skills to bring those numbers to life. His lifetime .302 batting average (sixty-five points lower than Cobb's) notwithstanding, Rose was the one player with the wherewithal to take up the quest.

Although he ended up playing in many more games, and accumulating far more at-bats, than did Cobb, Rose had earned the ethical right to go after the hits record by virtue of his incessant hustle, team-oriented success, a remarkable durability ideal for longevity, and a bevy of 200-hit seasons against better overall pitching and fielding than Cobb ever faced. Get this:

In one fifteen-year span of his career, from age twenty-four to thirty-eight, Rose rapped out 3,063 hits, an average of 204 a year, while batting .316.

⊏◯⊐

KAROLYN ROSE knew hardly anything about baseball when she met Pete in 1963, but by the time of the dissolution of their marriage years later, she knew almost as much about Ty Cobb as she did about her husband. It was a classic case of know one, know the other. Karolyn:

Pete is exactly like Ty Cobb, based on what I heard and read about Cobb. Except for one thing—Pete didn't drink. He never has, other than the occasional Scotch and water at an off-season party with friends, say, at New Year's. You can take my word that he never had more than two. He was never a drinker. Otherwise, he's the clone of Ty Cobb. No question about it.

⊏◯⊐

STAN MUSIAL's last season in the majors was Pete Rose's first. Stan the Man, who at the time was the National League's all-time hits leader (with 3,630), recalls one game in particular in which his Cardinals faced off against the Reds and he collected two hits, one to each side of the Reds' rookie second baseman. Pete, however, did him one better. Musial:

Pete got three hits that day. He was gaining on me right from the start.[1]

-=¤=-

PETE ROSE, *on comparing his hitting exploits with Ty Cobb's, as told to* Sports Illustrated's *Rick Reilly:*

I never said I was going to be the greatest hitter of all time. I just said I was going to have the most hits. Cobb's .367 average—that's untouchable. That's great. But if he was playing today, he'd hit .315, no doubt in my mind. Think about it. They never had any relief pitching back then. We get a fresh arm throwing against us every two innings sometimes. How tough could the pitching have been? You tell me how a guy is going to win 511 games (as Cy Young did). And did you ever see the gloves they used? They were about the size of a guy's hand. They had no padding at all. How many diving catches you think they made? I'm not saying Cobb was not a great player. I just think you're better off if you don't compare eras, okay?[2]

-=¤=-

MEL QUEEN, *one of Rose's teammates with the Reds in the sixties, remembers Rose as someone who could practically will himself to get more hits:*

Pete could really get the hits, especially when he really wanted them. There was one stretch in his career in which he'd had two straight years of two hundred hits or more, but in the third season, with only eight games left to go, he was sixteen hits shy of two hundred. I remember Pete saying, "I'm going to get my two hundred, you just wait and see."

And I said, "But, Pete, you have only eight games left. You've got to get two hits a game."

"Queenie, I'll do it."

"I hope you do."

I think he wound up with 204, or right around there. That's the kind of confidence he had in himself.

*Author **JAMES RESTON JR.** wrote this regarding Rose's pursuit of Cobb's record:*

As Rose approached Cobb's record, the comparisons were an endless source of heated discussion and amusement among fans, with Rose throwing himself into the debate with relish. With spitballs and dead balls, baseball, in Cobb's day, was a pitcher's game, and, before Babe Ruth, there were few home runs. But then the playing surfaces were inferior; spring training was a nightmare; the mitts were grotesque; and some of the top players in the nation, those who happened to be black, were barred from the majors. In Rose's time, the specialists, especially the relief pitchers, had arrived; most games were played at night, when it was harder to see the ball; the travel on the road was more taxing; and the pool of talented black players changed everything. "I had Willie Mays and Bobby Bonds chasing my stuff down," Rose said, resting his case.[3]

*Like Rose, **TONY GWYNN**, the longtime San Diego Padres star, was an expert when it came to hitting. Gwynn:*

I remember when Pete was forty years old. He kept talking about "catching Ty Cobb, catching Ty Cobb," and people said, "C'mon, you're forty! You can't catch Ty Cobb." Sometimes that's the kind of motivation you need to keep going.[4]

Rose's countdown to Cobb's record occupied almost the entire 1985 season for the Reds. As player-manager, Rose could insert himself into the lineup anytime he wanted, and his chase of Cobb came across as almost choreographed. Amazingly, Rose the manager kept his team on the cusp of NL West contention for most of the season. Fourteen victories in the Reds' last twenty games left them in second place, five and a half games behind the Dodgers. GLENN SAMPLE was the Reds' official scorer for Pete's 4,192nd hit, which came on September 11, a first-inning single off San Diego's Eric Show before 47,237 at Riverfront:

I was just looking forward to being a part of it. I never thought too much about it until I started getting some calls before the game, such as from a radio station in Canada. I got on the air with them one morning, and they said, "We hear you're going to be the official scorer for the game, and this is a big thing around the world."

Then I get a call from Dave Anderson, the Pulitzer Prize-winning guy from *The New York Times*. He said, "Hey, Glenn, I'm doing a story about Pete and the hit record, and do you realize how important this is? You might have to determine if it's a hit or error on a close call." I told him I hadn't given it much thought, that I was going to treat it like any other game I've ever scored. "If it's a hit, it's a hit; and if it's an error, it's an error," I said. "No big deal."

It dawned on me that scoring a hit or an error can involve a controversial call, which is very common in base-ball. You'll have some guy swearing that it's a base hit, and there will be other guys in the press box insisting that it's an error. Anderson said, "You know, as soon as you call it a hit, everyone will suddenly leave Cincinnati, leave the hotels and restaurants, and head for home. This thing will be over. But if it's an error and Pete gets no other hits, then about fifty thousand fans return the next day, and the hotels and restaurants stay full." Until then I had never looked at it that way, that it could come down to a controversial call and whatever decision I made could have huge economic implications.

I told Dave, "I'm not interested in money. I just enjoy the game, and I'm going to call it the way I see it." Fortunately, Pete got a solid hit, and it worked out great for everyone. I had never started feeling the pressure until I got those phone calls, and now I was relieved that it was all over. I probably got only three calls in all, but together they made an impact on me.

As a Cincinnati Enquirer *columnist,* **TIM SULLIVAN** *was part of the growing entourage that followed Rose from city to city, game to game, as he closed in on Cobb's record:*

There are a lot of little scenes that I remember. A lot of us were traveling with him for the last ten or fifteen hits. If he wasn't playing, there wasn't much to write, so we had to be pretty creative.

At one point, while we were in Saint Louis, I had learned that he wasn't going to be in the lineup one day. So I arranged to have a séance with Ty Cobb, with a woman medium in town. I went over to her house, and with a neighbor of hers there, too, the three of us conjured up Ty. So I got to interview Ty Cobb.

That ended up getting a lot of national play, although it turned out to be a much better idea than it was a story. The material just wasn't that good, and the woman obviously didn't know anything about baseball. Her answers were a little strange.

I also remember that day in Chicago where he was just two hits short and wasn't supposed to be in the lineup. But he ends up putting himself in the game when the scheduled starting pitcher, I think it was Steve Trout, gets scratched for some sort of bug. Back in the lineup, Pete gets two hits to tie the record.

PHOTO COURTESY OF CINCINNATI REDS

Rose reaches base again and his gesture tells it all—baseball's all-time hits leader.

What was interesting was, here was a guy who would be coming back to Cincinnati the next day to begin a homestand, where it was expected he would set the record. Now all of a sudden here he is, playing in an out-of-town game that he wasn't scheduled to be playing. There were reporters back in Cincinnati covering a Bengals game who were suddenly scrambling to get to Chicago when they heard that Pete would be playing after all. I think he got two more at-bats in that game after tying the record in which he could have broken the record.

That was Pete. He was more interested in getting the hits than in where he was when he got them. In retrospect, it's kind of hard to romanticize him, considering everything that has happened. But, to me, that was one of his finest hours, because he still was giving it his best shot regardless of the setting and popular sentiment.

SULLIVAN continues:

Another memory I have from "the tour" is how Rose didn't get any hits the first night back, and he didn't get the record-breaking hit until the next night, which I think was a Tuesday.

On one of those nights there was a press conference, and Pete was wearing this snap-up warm-up jacket. Someone asked a question like "How do you keep going?" or "What's the source of your staying power?" With perfect timing, he snaps open the jacket, and you see he has a Wheaties T-shirt on. He always had a great sense of timing and how to get a laugh.

The night he got the hit, he got it in the first inning. We had had all these plans about what the deadlines were going to be, and when he got the hit, the deadlines were moved up. It didn't really matter to me, because I had already written my column, a fairly short column, a kind of big-picture thing of all that was going on and what it meant. They wanted to keep it short so they could make a poster of the front page, without any of the front-page stories jumping.

After that, I had to write a second column about the whole night that ran inside. It consisted of a lot of little vignettes. He hadn't had any hits the night before, and Bruce Bochy, who was catching for the Padres (and later became the team's manager), was not normally in the lineup. He tells the story now of how he didn't think Pete could handle the fastball, from what he had seen the night before. So he wanted to see what would happen if he gave Pete a slider—to see if it would give him a chance to hit the ball—and of course he did.

⛆

SULLIVAN:

I believe there were a lot of circumstances in which Pete stuck his name in there (on the lineup card) to get the hit

record, although I've got to admit that the numbers indi-
cated that they were a better team when he was in the
lineup, whether he was hitting or not.

That first full year back, I remember writing a column
questioning whether be belonged in the lineup. I was scheduled to go on vacation soon after that, taking a trip to
Europe for the first time.

It was probably the first week in May of 1985, because I
was at the Kentucky Derby for a couple of days filing some
stuff. The radio shows were all over me, wondering how I
could write this.

Well, I was supposed to leave for Europe that Monday,
but I figured I needed to get out to the stadium Sunday to
give Pete a chance to see me and to say whatever he might
want to say in response to the column that had run a couple
of days earlier. I didn't want to bail on him completely.

We had it out for about twenty minutes, but it wasn't
anger on his part. He wasn't happy with it—he felt that I had
jumped the gun. I explained that he hadn't been very pro-
ductive and that I was justified in writing the column.

Anyway, I got on the plane the next day bound for
Europe for one of those packaged trips where you see ten
countries in twelve days. While I was gone, I would pick up
a *USA Today* or an international paper in Rome and Paris
and Munich, and every time I turn around, I see where Pete
has gotten two more hits. All of a sudden, his batting average had jumped from something like .230 to .280 or .290,
and I'm thinking, *I guess I really look like an idiot now.* After
I got back, he cooled off a little bit.

However, I did notice that the frequency of his extra-base
hits had really declined. His ability to really get around on the
ball and make meaningful contact had declined. It dawned on
me that I had never seen outfielders play so shallow on him.

SULLIVAN, *on the immediate aftermath of Rose's 4,192nd hit:*

I thought the aftermath of the hit was a little much. You know, with Marge Schott waving from the Corvette in right field. As much as that moment meant to a lot of people, it just didn't feel right to interrupt the game to hand the guy the keys to a car. I can remember Eric Show, the pitcher, sitting on the pitcher's mound, obviously tired of the delay and being exasperated with it.

I also remember that Pete cried, and I think a lot of people were surprised by that. He talked later about looking up into the sky and seeing his dad and Ty Cobb looking down on him. Whether he actually did, I don't know. Pete was pretty emotional. It was neat to see him and his son embracing, although I don't know if they were ever really that close.

⊏◇⊐

JERRY SPRINGER, *former mayor of Cincinnati, talks about the city's image and the effect Pete Rose's achievement had on it:*

This is a very successful city, with a highly skilled labor force, which is why we tend not to have the great dips and severe economic downturns that other cities do. And we don't have the density of poverty of most of the other big cities. It's also a very pretty city, with great restaurants, successful cultural institutions.

But none of this put Cincinnati on the map the way Pete Rose did. When he got that hit to pass Cobb, that was a very emotional moment in this city. It was "Look at us. We've got the best, the very best in history, right here in Cincinnati."[5]

7

GO DOWN GAMBLING

Although it had long been whispered that Pete Rose was getting more and more involved in gambling, it wasn't until several years after he had left the game as an active player that his gaming habits became a matter of public record. Rose's day of reckoning came in August 1989, when Baseball Commissioner Bart Giamatti announced that, as a result of an intense and detailed investigation, he had banned Rose for life from Major League Baseball. Giamatti's message to Rose: "Reconfigure your life." Nine days later, Giamatti died of a heart attack.

Perhaps as an incentive for Rose to mend his errant ways, Giamatti had written into the ban that Rose would be allowed to apply for reinstatement after one year. Rose waited until 1997 before writing a letter to Commissioner

Bud Selig seeking an open door back into baseball. Six years later, Selig still had not rendered a final declaration. Discussions between the two camps were continuing in 2003, and a possible compromise was considered that would at least allow Rose to become eligible for election to the National Baseball Hall of Fame.

Presumably, part of any such agreement would require an admission from Rose that he had bet on baseball games, something he had been unwilling to do since 1989. The evidence to the contrary is overwhelming:

In summary, baseball investigator John Dowd's 225-page report claims that between April 8 and July 3, 1987, alone, Rose made a total of 388 bets totalling more than $850,000. Fifty-two of the bets reportedly were on Reds games, albeit for the Reds to win each time.

⊏⊐

GLENN SAMPLE, *a lifelong Cincinnati resident, offers some perspective on why it was no random act of indulgence that Rose developed an interest in gambling:*

In the neighborhood in which he grew up, there were a lot of people who would bet on the horses and that kind of thing. Gambling was a part of the lifestyle. Gambling was a big thing back in the fifties, especially with there being a horse track right across the river in Kentucky. People would also bet on baseball, all kinds of things.

This all had to be in Pete's background, and he's probably been gambling for a long time. He couldn't help but gravitate toward that kind of thing. I lived five miles up the hill from him, and there was a lot of gambling going on up there as well. People could go into the back of a dry cleaners and put money down on some kind of action. That was very typical in that atmosphere back in those days.

TOMMY HELMS:

I must've gone to the track with Pete a hundred times, and I knew he liked to gamble and bet basketball and football. But that's his personal business. It wasn't any of my business.

I didn't know anything about the alleged baseball betting. I can't say I ever saw anything on his desk that might have been a hint that he was gambling.

When all this came down and he ended up getting banned from baseball, it was almost like a death or something. I just wish he could have gotten himself straightened out then. He could have gone to Gamblers Anonymous and in a short amount of time come back to managing. But it looked like he got to thinking that he was a little bit bigger than the game, and you can't get that way.

KAROLYN ROSE, *Pete's first wife, was well aware of his penchant for betting. After all, they had met at a racetrack:*

He always loved going to the track, either for the horses or the dogs. Even in spring training, we always went there.

I don't know if anyone has ever tried to get him to go to Gamblers Anonymous or to seek help. You've got to remember, he's Pete Rose—you never questioned him. In his own mind, he was a superstar, nothing could happen to him. I really believe that.

When he got banned, it was very sad for me and very sad for my two children. I cried. So did they. We knew how much he loved baseball. I believe if this hadn't happened to Pete, he would still be a manager. He will be a manager again someday, hopefully.

━◯━

*Sportswriter **BILL CONLIN** was among many in the fourth estate who picked up a whiff of Rose's interest in gambling long before the 1989 baseball investigation:*

The Phillies let Pete go after the 1983 season in large part because the commissioner's office had told them that Pete had a gambling habit. As it was, they had already taken all of the pay phones out of the clubhouse, followed by another one out in a tunnel outside the clubhouse door. There also was a pay phone up in the press box, where it was suspected that some radio guy was phoning in bets on Pete's behalf, and that phone was yanked, too.

What was ironic about all this is that the team president, Bill Giles, was also a big bettor. During spring training, a lot of guys would spend their spare time hanging out at Derby Lane, a greyhound racetrack in Saint Petersburg. It was a popular gathering spot. Bill Giles would be with one group of people in an upstairs suite, betting big-dollar amounts on the races, while guys like the ballplayers would be a couple of floors down. Bill and Pete would bet huge amounts, although I believe this is where Pete was getting in trouble with the IRS by not filling out 1099s on his earnings.

It became very obvious that Pete was a degenerate bettor, even though what he was doing was not yet prohibited. It was the action that appealed to Pete as much as the money. But the money became more of a factor when he was just managing the Reds and no longer playing and getting his four at-bats a game. To get that high-octane rush, he needed to find a substitute, and that's when he started betting bigger and bigger numbers, and he could have been in serious trouble considering who he was now dealing with. I believe his being Pete Rose is the only thing that kept him from ending up in an alley somewhere, beaten up.

⚊

JERRY SPRINGER, *the former Cincinnati mayor and at the time the city's top-rated news anchor, threw his support behind Rose in March 1989. This was as news of Rose's alleged gambling problem was starting to hit the streets, most prominently in a* Sports Illustrated *article:*

Sorry, I'm sitting this one out. I don't want any part of this posse chasing Pete's scalp. This time the lynch mob will have a riderless horse—mine. And it's not because I'm above it all, but rather, I still have a memory.

I remember what Pete's done for this town and for baseball, and for every kid who wore a fourteen on his jersey, slid headfirst into second at the local schoolyard pickup game, and who saw in Pete that you didn't have to be born with superior skills to make it in this world, that sheer hustle and determination and trying your best all the time was the real ticket to the top.[1]

⚊

JOHN DOWD, *a Washington, D.C., attorney hired by Major League Baseball as a special investigator to check out reports of Rose's rampant gambling, recalls how he got involved in the case:*

It was late February 1989, and I had just returned to my house from a trip to Atlanta. It was about ten-thirty at night when the phone rang. It was Fay Vincent, then deputy-commissioner-elect. He was with Bart Giamatti, president of the National League, and he wanted to know if I had any conflicts with the Cincinnati Reds and Pete Rose, and I said no.

I went and met with Bart, who I had never met before, and spent about forty minutes answering questions from him. When we got through, he asked, "Can you go to

Cincinnati in the morning?" I said sure. Then he sort of laid out some rules, saying that whatever I did, the world would see. He believed in complete transparency, no privileges. What ran through my mind was that whatever I did, it had to be perfect.

He wanted me to keep Pete's lawyers advised as to the progress of the investigation, even though that was nothing you normally did in an investigation. I told him I would do that, unless and until I felt someone might be obstructing the case. In fact, I did keep them apprised as to the progress of the case. And wherever the chips fell, they fell.

DOWD *would soon become a household name in living rooms where baseball fans congregated:*

At the time people were always asking me what I thought of Pete Rose—he was Charlie Hustle. I admired him. I'm someone who has always had to work very hard my whole life; I wasn't gifted, I'm not a fast thinker. Everything I've achieved, I've had to do the hard way. So, in that sense, I have something in common with Pete, and I admired him. I admire people who don't have talent and who work hard.

I had done investigations before. I had done the only investigation ever done of the FBI. I had done investigations all my professional life as a prosecutor. I told Bart (Giamatti) that all I cared about was that, whatever we did, he would be proud of it. It would be honest, airtight, and without leaks, and Pete would get a fair shake. Bart said that's all he wanted to hear. Indeed, there never was a leak. We interviewed some 110 people, and we interviewed many of them three times, even taking testimony to make sure that what they told us was right.

I headed to Cincinnati and met with my two wingmen. We proceeded to talk to (Paul) Janszen and his girlfriend, then some other people. As we interviewed people, we learned about others, and they were all Pete's friends. Mike Bertolini, Janszen, Tommy Gioiosa, the bookmakers—people that Pete hung out with. I didn't have a list when I flew out there, but we started to build one as we talked to people.

We were dealing with some unsavory people. My rule was, you don't believe them unless you can corroborate them. That was a rule that we had throughout. Within two weeks, we pretty much had the case locked. From the tapes and the documents we were given, then handwriting exemplars we took, some other things we had obtained, it looked pretty bleak for Pete. I shared all that with his lawyers, and they knew everything that I knew. I had no secrets from them.

I went about checking to see whether all this information I had would stand up. I went through telephone records, bank records, records with the Reds, records with visiting teams, hotel records—anything to determine whether this stuff would stand up.

There came a time when Bart—it was Bart's idea—said that we ought to take Pete's testimony, but in a nonconfrontational way. Give him a chance to look at it, see it, taste it, hear it. So a place was set up in a little convent outside Dayton, Ohio. The nuns couldn't have been sweeter. They always had these Krispy Kreme doughnuts and finger sandwiches for us to eat.

Pete and I spent two days talking to each other, and that essentially was his sworn testimony. We did it the way that Bart wanted us to do it, so that Pete could see everything that we had. The beauty of the way Bart designed it was that it was all straightforward, and that if Pete or his lawyers had anything to prove, that any of this or what the witnesses were saying was B.S. or that they were lying, then give it to us and we'll go talk to those folks. It was rare that anyone took us up on that offer to present suggestions or other ideas.

✦

*Once he and his troops had gathering all the evidence
and testimony,* **DOWD** *started sorting it all out:*

Opening Day was coming. Bart used to call me Saint John.
One night he called me and asked, "How's Saint John
doing?" And I said, "Saint John isn't doing very well." Two
of Pete's lawyers wanted to work it out, but his agent,
Reuven Katz, didn't want to budge.

That was too bad. I think the reason he (Katz) didn't want
to budge is that he had been so successful in getting Pete out
of one scrape after another over twenty years. A lot of stuff
had been swept under the rug. That was the arrogance we
were up against. I got along well with one of Pete's attorneys,
Roger Makely, though, and thought he was a good lawyer.

By the way, the U.S. Attorney overseeing all this told me,
"If you can settle this thing, I won't charge this guy. He'll
have to pay his tax bill, but he won't be charged with anything." I told Makely that, and he was thrilled. This would
have been a great result for a criminal lawyer. Then he said
to me, "Pete kind of likes you. Would you sit down and talk
to him, or take a walk with him through the woods or on a
beach somewhere and explain all this to him?"

I said, "I don't mind telling you, I think I can get on the
same page with Pete, and I think I can make him understand
the options he has." I said I would do it, and so I asked Bart
about it, and Bart said, "Go ahead." We agreed that it would
be totally off the record. We got the meeting teed up, but
then Katz vetoed that. So I never got that chance to have a
one-on-one with Pete.

I had even thought about taking him up to my house on
Cape Cod, someplace where nobody would be around,
nobody bothering anybody, and we could just talk. Pete is a
big street guy, and over the years you learn how to talk with

these guys. I figured after the two days of depositions that I would be able to talk with him. I think he thought I was fair, and I think we were fair. We weren't out to nail him, only to find out what the facts were.

Pete knew it was a dead-serious thing, that it was a capital-crime thing as far as baseball goes. But we never got to have that meeting, and that's the tragedy of it. I think we could have settled along the lines of him sitting out (of baseball) for five years. There's a lot to clean up here, and that's what I think the commissioner (Bud Selig) is facing now.

*One of Rose's accusers was **PAUL JANSZEN**, who in the eighties became close friends with Rose. He often spent hours a day at Rose's house, where Pete would sequester himself in the den surrounded by a forty-inch television set and two smaller sets, all tuned to different sporting events going on around the country. Janszen:*

Pete had an uncanny ability to follow all three at one time. He always watched the games and talked about what was happening. He was always active, always doing something. If there was a good play or if his team won, he'd jump up and give Tommy (Gioiosa) and me high-fives. Pete's wife, Carol, would just stay in the kitchen. If Pete lost on a game, he wouldn't be bothered unless the game was lost by a real dumb mistake. Then he'd be upset for five minutes. Otherwise, it was always, "Don't worry, we'll get even on the next game."[2]

In 1987 Janszen and his girlfriend Danita Jo Marcum accompanied Pete and Carol Rose to Tampa, for spring training, where they spent six weeks together.

Back home in Cincinnati, Janszen and Marcum spent a lot of nights at the Roses' house, and their get-togethers turned into sleepovers, with Paul and Pete staying up much of the night watching sports on satellite TV while Carol and Danita went upstairs to watch TV movies or look through Carol's closetsful of clothes. **JANSZEN:**

The funny thing that happened is that Pete started to need me around. I mean, he would get upset if I didn't go to his house at night after the Reds games. He would never say to me, "Hey, Paul, are you coming over tonight?" That wasn't in him. But he would have Carol say something to Danita, like, "Is Paul upset with Pete? Why doesn't he want to come over?" And she would say something like, "Carol, we've been over the last twenty-two nights straight. We would like to have a break." . . . He was lonely, that's what he was.[3]

JOE MORGAN, *Rose's Big Red Machine teammate, is believed to be one of a handful of former major-leaguers who have more than a superficial friendship with Rose. In his book* **Long Balls, No Strikes,** *Morgan had this to say about Rose's ban from baseball and his gambling problem:*

I'm often asked why Pete doesn't get it, why he is acting so self-destructively. People wonder why he can't at least pretend to be remorseful. The answer is as simple as it is complex. The thing that made Pete—whose physical skills were almost underwhelming—a great ballplayer was his transcendent confidence. That's what's killing him on this issue. Pete has always believed that, whatever the odds, he would always find a way to come out on top. He is convinced that he will eventually triumph. I'm telling him he can't win this thing on his terms. Pete can't see that because there's no quit in him. But perhaps it might help him if he knew how his peers viewed his predicament.[4]

*While **BILL LEE** isn't a part of Rose's inner circle, he does fall within one of the outer circles of people who care about Rose:*

For a lot of years we've been trying to get Pete to come up and play exhibition games with me in Canada, because it's a lot of fun. My catcher was Bobby Hull, the old hockey great. A lot of the old hockey players love to play baseball in the summer, and we do a lot of charity events together. Rose would have fit in nicely.

But Pete's gotten kind of cantankerous and doesn't like to play much anymore. He's just gotten the bitter attitude ever since he's been kyboshed from baseball. I feel sorry for him because, what's the big deal about betting? Everybody bets. Don Zimmer bets; all those guys from Cincinnati do. There's something about Cincinnati and that town just across the river from there—Covington, Kentucky—that's where all the gambling and bookies and stuff are.

The only bad thing in all this is that bookies can influence things. If they know that Rose is betting on a team, it's bound to influence things, although who's to say that Pete Rose is the best handicapper or best bettor in the world? He thinks he's good at betting, but he's not that good. He's a compulsive bettor, that's all. And compulsive bettors don't make the best handicappers. If he were betting on games involving the Reds, how would it look to bookies if Rose chose *not* to bet on his team to win? What would that tell you?

Gambling is part of life, and it shouldn't influence the outcome of a ballgame. However, when you start getting into things like shaving points or throwing games, then you have a real problem. Just the *process* of betting on a game shouldn't have any influence. As a manager, are you going to bet against your team and then make decisions to hurt them? I don't think so.

⊷⊷

Details of Rose's reported gambling indiscretions came out piecemeal in the spring and summer of 1989, as sportswriter **TIM SULLIVAN** *recalls:*

It came out in drips and drabs. At the paper, we were trying to figure out how to deal with it. Our guy traveling with the Reds and covering the team, Greg Hoard, was doing a lot of the work, but his time was divided between covering the team and digging up the story.

We also had a policy at that time that we couldn't quote anybody without using their name, so a lot of the same leaks that were being reported by other publications we couldn't use, even though we had them. So we were kind of hamstrung. When you're talking about bookmakers, investigations, and a lot of people who had axes to grind, you knew there was a lot being said that was not for attribution.

I don't know that any one publication dominated that story, but there were breaks in Cincinnati and New York, and *Sports Illustrated* did a lot of work and devoted a lot of man hours to it that no one else could afford to do.

As far as Pete was concerned, I remember having an interview with him in his office on the day that the story broke. He had been called to New York to testify. I tried to ask him in an indirect way about gambling, from the standpoint that someone in his position would have access to a lot of inside information. Wouldn't there be a temptation to trade on that? It was a fairly lengthy exchange, and my suspicions were certainly aroused at that point, although I still didn't know how deep it went.

I didn't think Pete would be stupid enough to bet on baseball, but I saw him as being capable of succumbing to that temptation. It was obvious to everyone that he was a pretty experienced gambler, but we all assumed it was just horses, dog racing, and pro football. It wasn't anything that would threaten his job directly.

I remember hearing that he had gone to Churchill Downs in Louisville and had arrived by helicopter in the infield. I thought, *This isn't the image that baseball wants. If you're going to go to the track, do it quietly.* I wrote a notes column one day that made mention that Pete might want to be more discreet or the commissioner might not take it too well, and it turned out to be a lot more prophetic than I realized at the time.

Sports columnist **DAVE KINDRED** *is one of America's best sports essayists when it comes to things like playing by the rules, and he makes a good point in withholding sympathy from Rose over his ban from baseball:*

Ever hear of William Cox? He owned the Philadelphia Phillies. He admitted that in the first two months of the '43 season, he bet on the Phillies to win. "Fifteen to twenty bets of from twenty-five dollars to one hundred dollars per game." Commissioner Kenesaw Mountain Landis banned Cox from baseball for life and forced him to sell the team.[5]

TIM SULLIVAN offers some memories regarding some of Rose's entourage during those late-eighties days of question:

Tommy Gioiosa was what was known as Pete's personal photographer, although I don't know what that really meant. He hung around Pete a lot and was selling a lot of memorabilia for him.

I didn't know (Paul) Janszen, although when the story started to break about Pete and his gambling, I got a call late one night from some guy who wouldn't identify himself, saying he had some dirt on Pete Rose. I told him I'd be willing to hear whatever he had to say, but he still wouldn't give me his name or any specific details. So I just kind of forgot about it.

It turned out later that it was Janszen who had called me. I know this because he came up to me soon after that and asked me if I remembered that phone call. I said, "That was you, huh?" And he said, "Yeah."

As far as I know, we didn't offer anybody any money to get the story, but I know we sure were looking for creative ways to get that story. At one point I said to one of our editors, "Can we arrange to buy this information as a screenplay, because the company I worked for, Gannett, had some kind of a relationship with Grant Tinker at that time." They ran it up the flagpole and came back and said no, but everyone knew that this was the white whale. Everyone knew that this was going to be the biggest story we had ever seen in Cincinnati.

As this book was going to press, Rose and his people were still working with Baseball Commissioner Bud Selig on a possible deal that would involve lifting Rose's lifetime ban from baseball. Attorney **JOHN DOWD:**

If you're going to let Pete back into the game, then he's got to go to every city and tell kids why betting is no good. It leads to debt, drugs, and stealing. It's pressure, a hassle that no one can live with. Pete's an addict, no different than an alcoholic. I know something about that, having taken a friend through alcohol treatment. He's in denial.

From my professional standpoint, this case has been exciting and challenging and all that, but it's a terrible thing. There have been tremendous efforts in the history of baseball to help people. But this guy had debts to the mob, he had connections to cocaine rings . . . it would have taken a lot of cleaning up. The beauty of baseball, the game, and the commissioner is that everybody wants to help him. There are doctors from Yale, etc., who had wanted to help the guy. We all wanted to help him.

He would have been a massive cleanup effort, and all it would have taken to get things going was for Pete to say, "I screwed up and I've been out of the game, and now I want to get back into the game. I want to straighten my life out." The problem is, he didn't have any advisors with the guts to tell him that.

Saint John had failed. The thing that shocked me in all this was how Pete didn't have any *really good* friends who would have been the type of guys to tell him to get some help, to come clean. A little later I ran into Bill White at the airport in Cincinnati—he was the president of the National League at the time—and told him that I failed, that I couldn't get anywhere with Pete. I said, "Bill, you played ball when he was playing ball. We've got to get to some of his friends and see if they can influence him and go around these lawyers." Bill looked at me and said, "Dowd, Pete hasn't got any friends in baseball."

I'm telling you, when I heard that, it about knocked me over. I had to sit down. I was shocked. As you pursue that, you find out that this guy hardly ever had a meal with his teammates and never really hung out with them. He hung out with the Gold's Gym guys and those folks. That's when you start to think that this guy is irreparable. I talked to Sparky Anderson, and he told me, "I love him like a son, but he can't stand me." Can you imagine that? I mean, a lot of those other guys on the Reds had no use for the guy.

During baseball's investigation of Rose in 1989,
TOMMY HELMS stood by his manager boss:

I would try to go and talk to him every now and then
because I thought he might be down on things, but he was
always upbeat. You can imagine what he went through. We
couldn't get off a bus or plane or eat somewhere without
there being a bunch of TV people and photographers around
us—tripods sitting outside restaurants while we tried to eat.

He had to go into a shell just to keep from being bothered
by everybody. One safe haven was the ballpark, where
reporters weren't allowed access at certain times. That was
tough, every day. We would have a traveling group of people
following us around everywhere, every day. Every TV network.

Sometimes there were so many people around that you
couldn't go through your normal pregame activity. It had to
affect the team on the field. Plus it seemed like everybody on
the team was getting hurt that year.

Commissioner Bart Giamatti's announcement of Rose's
ban came on August 22, 1989, in New York, and
Cincinnati Enquirer sports columnist TIM SULLIVAN
was there, barely in time:

My wife had just come back to work after maternity leave. I
came home and heard that there was going to be a press conference in New York. There was like one more flight out of
Cincinnati that night that would allow me to get there on
time for the press conference. I called my editor and he told
me to go.

By the time I landed in New York, the story had wild
cards everywhere. I called my office, while in the process of

writing my column that I needed to file, and they told me that *Nightline* was looking for me. As I was leaving the studio after doing the show, all the morning shows were lined up to get me on the next morning. I agreed to do one of them. I didn't know what the protocol was, that if I did one I had to do the others, or if I did one I couldn't do the others. I ended up spending the morning being shuttled around to all these shows, in essence representing Cincinnati just because I happened to be in New York.

Actually, I did one, went to the press conference, then did another one. What struck me at the press conference was how eloquent Bart Giamatti's remarks were. I think he realized that these remarks were going to be remembered and perhaps define his career. This was a guy who was a brilliant academician and essayist, and what people would remember best about him is that he's the guy who banished Pete Rose.

I got in one question at the press conference, and it was something to the effect of "Are you satisfied that this is the extent of baseball's gambling issue, and are there any other players involved, because I heard that there were?" The position then was that this is as far as it goes.

I didn't get a chance to speak to Pete that day, and I can't remember how long it was before I was able to run into him again.

*On August 24, two days after announcing Rose's banishment from baseball, Commissioner **BART GIAMATTI** explained the reasons for his decision in a prepared statement:*

The banishment for life of Pete Rose from baseball is the sad end of a sorry episode. One of the game's greatest players has engaged in a variety of acts which have stained the game, and he must now live with the consequences of those acts. By choosing not to come to a hearing before me, and by choosing not to proffer any testimony or evidence contrary to the evidence and information contained in the report of the Special Counsel to the Commissioner. Mr. Rose has accepted baseball's ultimate sanction, lifetime ineligibility.

This sorry episode began last February when baseball received firm allegations that Mr. Rose bet on baseball games and on the Reds' games. Such grave charges could not and must never be ignored. Accordingly, I engaged and Mr. (Peter) Ueberroth appointed John Dowd as Special Counsel to investigate these and other allegations that might arise and to pursue the truth wherever it took him. I believed then and believe now that such a process, whereby an experienced professional inquires on behalf of the Commissioner as the Commissioner's agent, is fair and appropriate. To pretend that serious charges of any kind can be responsibly examined by a Commissioner alone fails to recognize the necessity to bring professionalism and fairness to any examination and the complexity a private entity encounters when, without judicial or legal powers, it pursues allegations in the complex, real world.

Baseball had never before undertaken such a process because there had not been such grave allegations since the time of Landis. If one is responsible for protecting the integrity of the game of baseball—that is, the game's authenticity, honesty, and coherence—then the process one uses to protect the integrity of baseball must itself embody that integrity. I sought by means of a Special Counsel of proven professionalism and integrity, who was obliged to keep the subject of the investigation and his representatives informed about key information, to create a mechanism whereby the integrity we sought to protect was itself never violated. Similarly, in writing to Mr. Rose on May 11, I designed, as is my responsibility, a set of procedures for a hearing that would have afforded him every opportunity to present statements or testimony of witnesses or any other evidence he saw fit to answer the information and evidence presented in the report of the Special Counsel and its accompanying materials.

That Mr. Rose and his counsel chose to pursue a course in the courts rather than appear at hearings scheduled for May 25 and then June 26, and then choose to come forward with a stated desire to settle this matter is now well known to all. My purpose in recounting the process and the procedures animating that process is to make two points that the American public deserves to know.

First, that the integrity of the game cannot be defended except by a process that itself embodies integrity and fairness;

Second, should any other occasion arise where charges are made or acts are said to be committed that are contrary to the interests of the game or that undermine the integrity of baseball, I fully intend to use such a process and procedure to get to the truth and, if need be, to root out offending behavior. I intend to use, in short, every lawful and ethical means to defend and protect the game.

I say this so that there may be no doubt about where I stand or why I stand there. I believe baseball is a beautiful and exciting game, loved by millions—I among them—and I believe baseball is an important, enduring American institution. It must assert and aspire to the highest principles— of integrity, of professionalism, of performance. Of fair play within its rules. It will come as no surprise that like any institution composed of human beings, this institution will not always fulfill its highest aspirations. I know of no earthly institution that does. But this one, because it is so much a part of our history as a people and because it has such a purchase on our national soul, has an obligation to the people for whom it is played—to its fans and well-wishers—to strive for excellence in all things and to promote the highest ideals.

I will be told that I am an idealist. I hope so. I will continue to locate ideals I hold for myself and for my country in the national game as well as in other of our national institutions. And while there will be debate and dissent about this or that or another occurrence on or off the field, and while the game's nobler parts will always be enmeshed in the human frailties of those who, whatever their role, have stewardship of this game, let there be no doubt or dissent about our goals for baseball or our dedication to it. Nor about our vigilance and vigor—and patience—in protecting the game from blemish or stain or disgrace.

The matter of Mr. Rose is now closed. It will be debated and discussed. Let no one think that it did not hurt baseball. That hurt will pass, however, as the great glory of the game asserts itself and a resilient institution goes forward. Let it also be clear that no individual is superior to the game.[6]

JOHN DOWD, *in an excerpt from the Dowd Report that he presented to Giamatti:*

. . . Pete Rose has denied under oath ever betting on Major League Baseball or associating with anyone who bet on Major League Baseball. However, the investigation has developed information to the contrary. The testimony and the documentary evidence gathered in the course of the investigation demonstrated that Pete Rose bet on baseball, and, in particular, on games of the Cincinnati Reds Baseball Club during the 1985, 1986, and 1987 seasons.

The evidence showed that with few exceptions, Rose did not deal directly with bookmakers but rather placed his bets through others. As discussed in section III, during the 1985 and 1986 seasons, Rose placed bets on baseball with Ron Peters, a bookmaker in Franklin, Ohio. Although Rose placed his bets with Peters primarily through Tommy

Gioiosa, on several occasions Rose placed bets on baseball games, including Cincinnati Reds games, directly with Peters. Rose's dealings with Gioiosa, and ultimately with Peters, are corroborated by the testimony of others and by Rose's own financial records as well. Rose admitted placing bets with Gioiosa on football and basketball games, but denied placing any bets on baseball games.

When contacted by the author to look back on the Rose case from the perspective of fourteen years elapsed, JOHN DOWD offered the following:

I came to appreciate the force of this game, how much it is a part of the fabric of this country. You can imagine how many people have communicated to me over these last fourteen years, and I would say that ninety-nine and forty-four hundredths percent of them have been polite.

I was part of Bart's and Fay Vincent's efforts to keep the game honest. I don't know where the game is today because we haven't had a cop on the beat for a while, but I guarantee you that Bart and Fay were good cops. I had players call me and tell me that they stopped betting after the Rose case. Lenny Dykstra stopped—he said it scared the hell out of him.

In all these cases involving gambling, whether it's baseball or not, drugs were involved. I never knew that, even though I had been a strike-force prosecutor, although I dealt more in corruption and fraud. I don't remember gambling ever having this connection to drug operations. This is frightening. In gambling, you're not only dealing with debt and corruption of the game, but you're also dealing with narcotics.

I probably should have just retired in 1989 and been a happy soul. I really believed we helped the game, and I believe it's still helping today by reminding people of the importance of what Bart did (in banning Rose from baseball). This country has been through a time where ethics and honesty and truth don't mean anything. I think we're coming out of this valley, but this game of baseball will not survive if it's not an honest game.

The other thing is, my heart sort of bled for the people of Cincinnati. They were very, very nice to me. They are great baseball fans out there.

PETE ROSE's ban from baseball wasn't the end of his problems. Just a year later, in 1990, he was convicted of tax invasion for failing to report income of $350,000 earned between 1984 and 1987 from gambling, autographs, personal appearances, and the sale of memorabilia. He was sentenced to five months in a federal facility for underpaying his taxes by $162,000. Following is the text from a ninety-second statement Rose made before U.S. District Judge S. Arthur Spiegel during his sentencing on tax-evasion charges:

Your honor, I would like to say that I am very sorry. I am very shameful to be here today in front of you.

I think I'm perceived as a very aggressive, arrogant type of individual, but I want people to know that I do have emotion, I do have feelings, and I can hurt like everybody else, and I hope no one has to go through what I went through the last year and a half. I lost my dignity. I lost my self-respect. I lost a lot of dear fans and almost lost some very dear friends.

I have to take this opportunity to thank my wife (second wife Carol) for giving me so much moral support during this ordeal. It had to be tough on her when your five-year-old son comes home from school and tells her that his daddy is a jailbird.

I really have no excuses because it's all my fault. All I can say is, I hope somewhere, somehow in the future I'm going to try to make it up to everybody that I disappointed and let down. Thank you very much.[7]

Note: Rose was sentenced to five months in a federal minimum-security prison followed by three months in a halfway house or community treatment center. The federal prison was located in Marion, Illinois, the birthplace of no less than Ray Fosse. The Ray Fosse Softball Field is about a mile away.

*Fellow sportswriter **TRACY RINGOLSBY**, then with the Dallas Morning News, covered Rose's sentencing:*

I remember thinking when I was there, *You know, everyone is going to be writing about the sentencing, but I need something other than that to write about to justify my being there.* Otherwise, we could have just taken the whole story off the wires.

I decided to check into what it was that he was going to have to do in terms of community work as part of his sentence. I think it was some sort of boys club, where he was supposed to talk to these kids. So I went there to talk to some of these guys about Pete Rose. What I remember is this guy taking me over there and telling me that, "This place is integrated. We don't only have black kids at this club, we've got the Appalachian whites." That's when I knew I was really in the South (Cincinnati is right across the Ohio River from Kentucky).

DICKIE NOLES, who played on the Phillies with Rose, remains undeterred by all that has happened:

You can't change my thoughts about Pete. Pete will forever be in my heart.

━◘━

*Prominent baseball-statistics analyst **BILL JAMES**
weighed in about ten years ago with his assessment of
Rose's predicament arising from the baseball ban:*

From 1963 to 1988, Rose was the subject of immense adulation from the nation's sportswriters, who wrote about what a great team player he was and what a great interview he was. I could never figure out why, beginning in 1989, the good things suddenly didn't count any more. It would help if some of those people and some of his old teammates would get out front now and take some of the flak for him.

In any case, I hope that Rose will soon be permitted to reenter the game, and I believe that he will. But you don't *begin* the rehabilitation of baseball's Wronged Man by putting him in the Hall of Fame. That's where you end it.[8]

8

"C," FOR COOPERSTOWN

B ecause of his lifetime ban from baseball, Rose remains ineligible for Baseball Hall of Fame consideration as of this writing. His absence in Cooperstown is easily the most conspicuous among others deserving of enshrinement, among them, Gil Hodges, Ron Santo, Jack Morris, and Bert Blyleven.

The general sentiment for many years has been that Rose's reinstatement to baseball would be a rubber stamp for his election to the Hall of Fame. That might no longer be the case. The longer an unrepentant Rose goes without confessing his betting sins, the more thumbs-down votes he could be accruing. Part of his problem, too, is that he continues to be spotted at racetracks in Las Vegas.

It's one thing to say one is repentant. It's another to say one is repentant and really mean it, in deeds as well as actions. Character remains a Cooperstown criterion, and Rose still has some 'splaining to do. Don't engrave his plaque just yet—there could be a backlash waiting in the wings. Look at what happened in Canada. Rose's brief stint in 1984 playing for the Montreal Expos made him eligible for the Canadian Baseball Hall of Fame, and he was nominated for election in January 2003. But once the balloting was complete, and although Rose reportedly had already cleared his schedule to appear at the induction ceremony, he didn't receive a single vote.

꘎

Pending the discussion of Rose's possible baseball reinstatement going on at the time this book was written, veteran Philadelphia Daily News *sports columnist* **Bill Conlin** *offered his thoughts on Cooperstown and Rose:*

I would vote for him going into the Hall of Fame but not reinstate him for active participation in the game.

All those hits have to have a home in Cooperstown. He got the hits, and he got them at a time when he wasn't betting on baseball and when he was still considered an icon of the game. But he doesn't belong managing a team or being paid to be a hitting coach or whatever. That's an appropriate punishment for the things he did after he ceased being a baseball player.

I remember when the noose was starting to close in around him in early 1989. I was among dozens and dozens of reporters around his office in Cincinnati one time when he got summoned to a meeting with his higher-ups. As he headed out of his office toward the elevator, a stampede of writers followed. There were maybe fifty to seventy-five writers following him and blurting out questions, just like one of those scenes you see in a movie. It reminded me of all those villagers chasing Frankenstein's monster. All they needed were the torches.

The elevator door opens and Pete steps in, and that's when he sees me and yells one of the best double negatives you will ever hear: "Bill Conlin, there ain't no way you ain't voting for me for the Hall of Fame."

TRACY RINGOLSBY, now with the Rocky Mountain
News *in Denver and another longtime baseball writer
with a Hall of Fame vote, presents a different way of
looking at Rose's Hall of Fame worthiness:*

Pete Rose is the perfect example of an addictive personality. You could see it just in the way he approached the game.

In general, we have a forgiving society, but he's lied about it publicly for so long that it's hard to forgive him. It's a sickness, an illness, but that doesn't make it right.

In some ways, I think he has made more money off the ban than he would have if there never had been a ban, or if it had been lifted earlier. He's also created some of his own problems in terms of perception, such as showing up at Cooperstown during the Hall of Fame Week and setting up his own big autograph session.

Rose just can't stay away from things—he has to be in the middle of everything. He can't stand not being the center of attention. On some level, he's aggravated his situation.

As a player, he deserves to be in the Hall of Fame. But there's more to being in the Hall of Fame than just what you accomplish in games. I don't have a problem with the fact that he's not eligible. I wouldn't campaign that he has to remain ineligible forever, but his absence from the Hall of Fame isn't something I would call a disgrace.

People debating the Hall of Fame issue will refer to this guy or that guy, comparing them to Rose, but times change, and when times change, our values do, too. Was Ty Cobb a racist? You know what? Racism wasn't considered the same thing back then that it is now. That was the environment, the mentality, that guys of Cobb's era grew up in. I'm not saying it's right, but you have to accept that different things are permitted at different times in history.

I'm confident that forty or fifty years ago, there was the same kind of stuff going on (players betting, etc.), but the public didn't want to know about the flaws of their heroes. So, is Rose being held to a higher standard than guys were forty or fifty years ago? Most likely, but our values have changed, too, in terms of what we expect from people.

What about drunken driving? Hey, you can go to prison for that now. It used to be kind of a joke with many people. As a society we have gotten more demanding, with a lower threshold on some things to the point of being ridiculous. Then there are other changes in perception like that, such as with drunken driving, which I think are pretty good. Pete created his own problems in that regard.

Rose's high school classmate **ED BRINKMAN**, *who, by the way, played for three different teams managed by Billy Martin, supports Pete's bid for the Hall of Fame:*

I feel in my heart that he should be in the Hall of Fame. As far as the other part is concerned, I'll let someone else worry about that. I really don't know much about that, nor have I read much about it.

BOB HOWSAM, *former Reds general manager:*

Under the right circumstances, I would have hoped that Pete Rose would be in the Hall of Fame. No more explanation needed, except I don't think you should reward people for breaking the rules or breaking laws. I'm proud of the fact that four other men from that Big Red Machine team are in the Hall—Johnny Bench, Joe Morgan, Tony Perez, and Sparky Anderson.

Former pitcher **JACK BALDSCHUN,** *part of whose career overlapped with Rose and the Reds:*

I don't think he should get into the Hall of Fame, just from the standpoint that he bet on baseball. It's against the rules. Enough said. Even if he turns around and admits he bet on baseball, he's still only putting his foot in his mouth, because that admission would still be an admission of something that is clearly against the rules of Major League Baseball. Everybody else has to abide by those rules, why should he be any different?

As far as playing with or against Pete, there are other stories that I could relate, but I won't because they are really bad. If you're going to let him into the Hall of Fame, then I think you ought to let Joe Jackson in.

In his 1999 book Long Balls, No Strikes, **JOE MORGAN** *made this open plea to Rose:*

C'mon, Pete, you need to do some fence-mending here. If you think you've made enough apologies, then one more won't hurt. Unlike Joe Jackson, you never threw a baseball game; you loved winning too much to do that. . . . I think baseball would be a better game for your presence. You're the living embodiment of hustle, you can teach hitting to anyone, and you were once one of our game's best ambassadors (Pete could talk baseball for hours to a stump.)

Admit your mistakes, say you're sorry, and give the country, the writers, and the Hall a chance to embrace you once again. I'm not guaranteeing they'll do it, but I do think it's your last best shot.[1]

⋯

Sports columnist **DAVE KINDRED,** *writing in* The Sporting News:

Early gleanings from sportswriters who vote in the Hall of Fame elections indicate Rose would be a first-ballot selection. In that case, here are two suggestions for the Cooperstown folks: Inscribe on Rose's plaque a sentence describing his betrayal of the game; and hang his plaque under the cover of night, doors closed, no ceremonial pomp.[2]

⋯

BILL JAMES, *analyzing Rose's exclusion from the National Baseball Hall of Fame:*

Pete Rose isn't banned from baseball because he's a bad person. He's banned from baseball because he broke the rules. As (Hall of Fame library historian) Tom Heitz says, the problem with Pete Rose isn't that he gambled. The problem is that he broke the rule against gambling.

Think of Pete Rose as being in a baseball prison. Suppose that we applied the same slipshod argument to those who broke the rest of our rules. Should we, in order to send anyone to prison, have to prove that everyone else who isn't in prison is a saint? Of course not. But what would happen if, before we could send anyone to prison, we would have to show that he was a bad person, that he was a worse person than all of the other people who aren't in prison? It wouldn't work, would it? That doesn't have anything to do with it. You don't go to prison for being a bad person. You go to prison for breaking the rules.[3]

✦

BILL LEE, the Spaceman:

One thing about Pete that was so special was his longevity, just like Carl Yastrzemski. Remember, Yaz and Cal Ripken both wore the number eight, which, when on its side, looks like the symbol for infinity. Those were two of the most durable players who ever played the game. There's something about that number—Yogi Berra, he had it, too. Gary Carter. You know, a lot of eights make it to the Hall of Fame.

Pete pushed and pushed, and just kept on going. Hopefully, things will change, and eventually guys like Pete and Buck Weaver (of the 1919 Chicago "Black" Sox) will make it into the Hall of Fame. I say, "What the hell? Let everybody into the Hall of Fame."

There are so many guys who not only made it into the majors but were able to forge out a career. And so many of those guys were so good and right on the edge of Hall of Fame consideration. Guys like Luis Tiant, Bert Blyleven, Sparky Lyle, Goose Gossage, Ron Santo still have not gotten in. Finally, they let Bill Mazeroski in. Gary Carter, too. It's just a big political football.

✦

MEL QUEEN, another former Reds pitcher and Rose teammate:

Pete Rose deserves to be in the Hall of Fame. That said, he could have handled the gambling situation differently. But what he's done for baseball is incredible. He's a fabulous guy for baseball, and he has accomplished so many things.

✦

RICHARD HAUCK, *one of Rose's coaches from his days*
at Western Hills High:

Pete's a local boy who made good and has had problems, and
it seems like people support individuals who have problems.
They can be very, very forgiving, and I know that most people in Cincinnati would love to see him in the Hall of Fame.
But I don't think the rest of the country necessarily wants to
see that. I don't know. It might be true that people like for
their heroes to have flaws. People with flaws seem to get all
the publicity. Look at Mike Tyson.

BUD HARRELSON, *one of a number of former players*
with possible cause to be embittered against Rose:

For years I said, "What's up with this?" The guy's a great
player, and it was really hard to believe that he had actually
done everything that he had been accused of. But he made
the deal, and the longer it went (before there was any serious talk about his being reinstated), I said to myself, *They*
must have a lot on him. My heart says to put him in, but I
don't know the extent of the issue.

9

ROSE REDUX

So much of what can be said about Pete Rose goes off in many different directions. Some of it is good, some bad. He is one of those rare American sports figures who is beloved by a large part of the population, despised by another, and to everyone a lightning rod for controversy. Others in this category who quickly come to mind are Bob Knight, Howard Cosell, and Woody Hayes. Part of what has made each so intriguing as a public figure is, on the one hand, incredible success in his chosen field; on the other, a certain dark side.

As with those others, there is a great dichotomy in Rose's makeup and actions. On the field, he's an unrivaled role model; off it, his indiscretions disqualify him as a role model. Selfish with his stats, yet giving to those less fortunate. Great with the media, but remaining at arm's length from those who call him friend. By no means an intellectual, yet in possession of a genius baseball IQ. Diligent with his work habits in the batting cage, but sloppy in the betting way.

Pinning Pete down is as about as easy as holding him up at third on a single to center. Still, many have tried. Judge him for yourself.

✦

DAVE BRISTOL:

Pete has an amazing memory, but I never saw him write anything down. He could remember pitches that pitchers had gotten him out on long before. It was almost like a photographic memory, and all the stuff he remembered so well wasn't just about him. He could tell you a lot about what other guys were doing. He made it his business to remember stuff like that.

Pete had to be a joy to writers because he always had good stuff he could lay on them. Always. Even with all the stuff that he was being asked about in '89, I don't remember ever seeing him get mad or walk off in the face of the questions about gambling. He wouldn't even use the "No comment" line. He always had something to say and wouldn't blow anybody off. If you were writing about baseball, he was always ready for you.

✦

PATRICIA BLUM:

After Pete became famous, everyone sort of lost touch with him. One thing I remember is how he would often come back—he loved the Western Hills area—and cruise the area. There was a restaurant in Cheviot that he used to go to all the time. It was a place called the Gay Nineties. He would be cruising around in his Rolls Royce, and that was a sight, because we knew who he really was.

I just wonder how many people from Western Hills *really* knew him well.

⌑

GEORGE WILL, *in a June 27, 1991, column entitled*
"The Collision Between Bart and Pete":

When he was getting divorced (from Karolyn), he was asked if it upset him. "Nothin' bothers me," he said. "If I'm home in bed, I sleep. If I'm at the ballpark, I play baseball. If I'm on the way to the ballpark, I worry about how I'm going to drive. Just whatever is going on, that's what I do."[1]

⌑

KAROLYN ROSE, *wife number one:*

I fell in love with him on our third date. Where did we go for that date? The ballpark. Let's face it, I was getting ready to marry a walking-encyclopedia-of-baseball player.

He's a self-made man. He loves stats. I enjoyed it, and from him I was able to learn the game and meet so many neat and wonderful people. One time President Gerald Ford came into Cincinnati, and Pete, Tony Perez, and I got to meet him. He shook my hand and said to me, "Your husband sure knows how to hit those home runs."

"Ohhhhh," I said, "you must be talking about Perez. All *my* husband hits are singles and doubles."

He said, "I'm so sorry, Mrs. Rose."

I also got to meet Joe DiMaggio, as well as a lot of other superstars at that time. I think it was at a banquet in New York that we met Joe, and he and Pete became pretty good friends. They once did a USO tour to Vietnam together. They were there for something like twenty-eight days, maybe even a little bit longer.

I can remember Pete talking about the trip, about how in

going over there they landed on an aircraft carrier. Pete said it was unbelievable. Then they went into the jungles of Vietnam and got to meet guys in their foxholes. Pete told me it was almost a surreal experience. These soldiers would look up and see Pete and Joe and wonder if they were dreaming. They couldn't believe these two great baseball players were actually there with them in the jungles of Vietnam. They rarely saw anybody, sometimes months at a time, other than the guys in their units. They couldn't believe what they were seeing.

I remember Pete telling me that he and Joe were given military ranks, and soldiers were told to address them as "Lieutenant" or "Colonel" or whatever rank they had. This was because otherwise they risked being captured and killed by the Viet Cong as spies. Pete really enjoyed going over there to meet the guys. "You can't believe how high their morale was to see Joe DiMaggio," Pete told me. "They couldn't understand what we were doing there, and I just explained to them that we were there to visit them." It was a pretty emotionally intense experience.

I think that's one of the best things that Pete ever did, and doing it with Joe DiMaggio—oh, my goodness, Joe had to be one of Pete's idols.

⊏◊⊐

More from KAROLYN:

One time when we were dating, Pete called me at home, and my brother Fred answered the phone. When Fred came to get me, he said, "It's Pete Rose on the phone. He's 'Hot-dog,' that's what they call him. He's a hot-dog."

"He is?" I said.

"Yeah, and he's going to be a great baseball player."

⊏◊⊐

TOMMY HELMS:

I remember one time when we had to do some kind of TV-promotion thing in California. Pete, Al Ferrara of the Dodgers, and I went up to Del Mar from San Diego, and we got to ride in a limousine that they sent by for us. We ended up taking the limo to the track in Del Mar, and we all got busted there. We didn't have any money coming back.

The driver took us back to San Diego, to the stadium, and because we didn't have any money for tips, we tried to give him some tickets, but he wouldn't go for that. I'm the only one who had a credit card on him, so we used that to tip the driver. I think I gave him seventy-five dollars. The good thing about that was that he had one of those devices in his car where he was able to accept credit cards.

LARRY STARR, *the former Reds trainer, compares Rose to Elvis Presley:*

I'm a big fan of Elvis, and I'm reading this book on him . . . called *Are Your Lonesome Tonight?* And it's scaring the hell out of me. People who reflect back on Elvis Presley now say, "Who were his friends? Where were they when he was taking all these drugs? Where were they when he was not sleeping?" So much of it reminds me of Pete Rose. The more powerful men are, the more difficult they are to reach. They dominate you. If you try to help them, they fend you off.[2]

GEORGE WILL, *in an April 2, 1989, column titled "Pete Rose's Chromosomes":*

Rose has baseball in his chromosomes. Tell him Lindbergh flew the Atlantic in 1927 and he responds, "The year Ruth hit sixty." To you, 1941 means Pearl Harbor; to Rose, 1941 means DiMaggio hitting in fifty-six consecutive games and Williams hitting .406. A statistician once tried to stump Rose with this arcane question: What active player has the highest ratio of flyouts to groundouts? Rose replied, "Easy. Gary Redus." Rose was right.[3]

⊲✧⊳

BILL LEE, on Rose as a throwback:

There have always been guys who weren't enamored of Pete, but now he also has that stigma on him as far as being a gambler and everything else. You don't want your kids to grow up and be that hind of overachiever.

In today's world, you no longer have any players with true character or with distinctive color, like what Pete Rose was. Now we've got guys surrounded by agents and whatnot who do all of the speaking for the guy. There are no longer poets of the game because agents and lawyers ghostwrite everything. Everything is all about legalese and not wanting to say anything that will hurt yourself, anything that is politically incorrect. Everybody treads on their words. It's boring.

Pete Rose is still verbose. You get a few beers into him and he's a great guy to talk to about the game because he knows it and he loves it and he played it. He's one of us. We all belong to a unique fraternity, and it's a very small group of us. We were guys who were out there and were genuine and honest, and were our own people. We all had our own individual nicknames and our own little mystiques, and now you have more brain surgeons out there than you do genuine ballplayers.

Pete's a fifties guy, the epitome of what we picture when we mention "Joe Jock." He even had the butch haircut. He did everything fast, and you would see him with the big T-bird or the souped-up Plymouth Duster. He's right out of *American Graffiti*, maybe even before that.

He's almost in-between generations. He's not the hippie—he's almost anti-hippie in a way—and he wasn't quite old enough to go to Korea and fight. He was always tough, and he'll always be tough.

❦

Ross Grimsley:

He was the same off the field as he was on. Sometimes he would rub people the wrong way, and he could be arrogant at times, but all in all, he treated the rest of us, his teammates, pretty well. Even years later, after a lot of time had gone by, I would run into him and he was always friendly with me, so I can't say anything bad about him. He treated me right. Reggie Jackson was the same way.

Both of those guys have done things for me they didn't have to do. Here in Baltimore we used to have a sports banquet to honor ballplayers, such as the area's minor-league player of the year, and one year they asked me to call Pete and see if he would come over so they could give him one of their awards. I called him, and he said he was going to be up in Atlantic City doing something. They helicoptered him down here to Baltimore, and he showed up.

A friend of mine was sitting in the front row, while Pete was up on the dais, and my friend was there with his mother, who had Alzheimer's. I asked Pete to come down and say hi, and he came down and spent some time with them, signing some stuff for them as well. He didn't have to do that, and I thought it was pretty neat that he did.

❦

Mel Queen:

One time at minor-league spring training in Tampa,, we were playing a game of pepper. Pete noticed that there were three bigwig executives—Gabe Paul, Phil Seghi, and a third guy I can't remember, up in the stands—and Pete's hittin'. He says, "Hey, Queenie, throw me a ball high." I said, "Why?" He said, "I'm going to scatter them up there. I'm going to hit a line drive right at them"

I flipped it up there, and Pete hit a bullet, sending those guys ducking.

⎯◇⎯

JIM WIETHOLTER, *one of Rose's Western Hills schoolmates:*

Here's a bit of sports trivia about Western Hills High School that's interesting. If you were to ask who was the most famous athlete to come out of there around that time, you would probably say Pete Rose, of course. But to many people around the world, that's not the correct answer.

Roland Muhle, who later changed his last name to Mullen, was a swimmer in high school and went on to participate in four Olympics in flat-water canoeing. True story. He graduated high school with Pete Rose, and there were many people in the world who knew who Roland Mullen was and had never heard of Pete Rose. Yet, people in Cincinnati had never heard of Roland. He worked out in his garage in an above-ground pool with a boat tied off to one end of the garage with inner tubes.

Talk about drive. This guy had drive! I don't think he and Pete even knew each other, although I know about Roland because I was on the Western Hills swimming team with him.

⎯◇⎯

RICHARD HAUCK, *a Western Hills coach in the Rose era, and beyond:*

Recently (early 2003), we had a Western Hills Sports Stag, where all the guys who have played sports at the school are invited back for a get-together, with some speakers. It's a way to raise money for the school.

This time Jim Frey and Don Zimmer were the main speakers. Some gal helping to organize the stag called to ask me if I would invite Pete. I was able to get a cell phone number for Pete and called him and left a message but didn't hear back from him for a while.

Finally, I get a call from Pete and explained the situation to him, that we were having this sports stag and that Zimmer and Frey were the main speakers. At that point, Pete said, "Well, you don't need me then." I told him that it would still be nice if he would come, but that it wouldn't bother me either way. He didn't come. He said he would come to the school's seventy-fifth anniversary celebration in the fall (2003), and I told him I would send him the information when I got it.

Another time we tried to induct him into the Heightsville Old-timers Hall of Fame. Every time we have one of these, about three hundred people come out to watch us induct three or four new members. This is something we started way back when, in the thirties. We induct guys who played ball in this area, whether high school ball, Knothole Baseball, or whatever. Some of us tried to get ahold of Pete, and all we could get were his lawyers. They wanted to know how much he was going to get. We said, "This is a voluntary thing and we don't pay anybody." So Pete's not in that Hall of Fame.

⊏○⊐

HAUCK, on a softer note:

I remember one time seeing Pete at a local basketball game and his saying to me, "You know, if it wasn't for baseball, that would be me out there." And he was pointing at the guy pushing the mop down the floor. "That's about all I can do other than baseball." Baseball was his thing.

-⊏◯⊐-

GLENN SAMPLE, *another of Cincinnati's native baseball*
sons:

In addition to being the Reds' official scorer, I used to do other things for them—such as when the team went on the road, I would sometimes catch a pitcher left behind to rehab from an injury. So that gave me a chance to work with some of the Reds pitchers. I didn't get paid, but I was just happy to do it.

One year, after Pete signed with the Phillies, we had a baseball strike. Reuven Katz, an advisor to Pete and a prominent Cincinnati attorney, gave me a call and said, "Hey, Glenn, I just got a call from Pete, and he wants to know if he can come over and take batting practice on your field tomorrow (when Sample was still coaching baseball at the University of Cincinnati). He doesn't want to get behind on his hitting during the strike." I said that would be great.

Next day, Pete was out there practicing with our team. He got in there and hit for about an hour, and our kids were just thrilled to have him there. By this time, Pete was a big star and the Big Red Machine was in full gear. Some of our pitchers throwing to him were worried more than anything, afraid that they might accidentally hit him with a pitch and hurt him. But they all did a pretty good job pitching it to him, and no one hit him with a pitch.

Pete put on a real show for my players, spraying the ball all over the place, and it really gave all my guys a great work-out in the field. We must have had close to a thousand people stop by and watch practice once word got around that he was out there practicing with us. Pete would foul off some pitches over a fence, and the kids would scramble to retrieve the ball so that they could bring it by after practice for him to sign. And he readily complied.

⊏◇⊐

JOHN DOWD, *on the two days he spent interviewing Rose during his investigation:*

What struck me is that he's bigger than I had thought he was. When he was playing baseball, especially at bat, he was always crouched down. I was also struck by the thickness of his build. I don't think he was still in playing shape at the time, but he's still a powerful guy.

He was easy to get along with, very polite. I was worried because he had flown overnight from Los Angeles. He said he was fine. I told him we could knock off until noon so that he could get some sleep, or we could start the next day, but he said no, that he'd be fine.

It wasn't difficult, it wasn't awkward. We got along. I showed him everything, but I tell you what, when I showed him those betting slips and played some tapes that his middleman had made of them talking to each other, he turned green. I wish I had videotaped it. It hit him. He didn't know how to answer it. He knew we were hitting home.

He wasn't fidgety. He sat there, but when he got nervous, he just talked a lot. Still, he was a complete gentleman at the time, which shows you that he can behave. He knows how to handle himself when he has to. We didn't have a cross word the whole time. The only thing I saw at all was when one of his attorneys, Roger Makely, tried to interrupt him at one point with a doughnut in his mouth, and Pete told him, "Shut up, I'm trying to talk to John." We just took our time, and it wasn't confrontational. No games. No tricks. No setups. No nothing.

PHOTO COURTESY OF MONTREAL EXPOS

Although Rose would not complete a full season with the Montreal Expos, he gave his Canadian fans some terrific moments.

JIM O'TOOLE, *on Rose's rapport with sports reporters:*

Pete pretty much had his way with most of them. He would talk baseball all night long with these guys if they wanted him to.

ED BRINKMAN:

On the back of my baseball card it had been written that I had been a high school teammate of Pete's, so people would see that and ask me all the time about what it was like to play with Pete back then. Funny thing, I have no idea if Pete's card mentioned me on the back. I never checked, but I already know his stats; they're pretty impressive. I try not to read mine.

TRACY RINGOLSBY, *now a baseball writer for the* Rocky Mountain News:

I can remember when I was working in Kansas City and he was with the Montreal Expos. I was in Florida during spring training and was working on a Pete Rose piece. I went to West Palm Beach to talk to him, and I found him in the batting cage. I walked up to him, told him who I was, and the next thing I know, he pulls up two milk crates to sit on and we talked for about an hour and a half. I was in awe of this because he didn't know me from Adam, just as some guy from a paper in Kansas City.

I also remember a winter or two later, when he was player-manager for the Reds, and he came to Kansas City for a card signing. He had with him Reds pitcher Tom Browning and another player I can't remember. The promoter told me that part of the deal in Pete's coming was that these two players had to come, too, and he gave part of his guaranteed appearance money to those two other players. He wanted not only to get them some money, but to expose them to another side of the big-league atmosphere.

MEL QUEEN:

Pete was very meticulous. One year in Cincinnati I lived for a while with him and his first wife, Karolyn, and I saw where Pete would line up all his alligator shoes outside the closet. One morning he woke up and got really upset because their air conditioner had leaked all over his alligator shoes. What did he do? He went out and bought some more.

RICHARD HAUCK:

One time in the early seventies, we took Pappy Nohr, the former baseball coach at Western Hills, up to Chicago for a get-together that also included Pete, Don Zimmer, Eddie Brinkman, Russ Nixon, and Jim Frey—all guys who had played ball for Pappy at Western Hills.

This was a great chance to get together and honor him, because it worked out that all those guys were in town. We took Pappy to a Reds-Cubs game and then out to get something to eat. At one point this kid came up to Pete and asked him for his autograph. Pete wouldn't give it to him.

The rest of us, seeing this, were upset with Pete. We couldn't believe it. Pete then told us that all the kid was going to do was get the autograph and take it across the street to some grown-up guy waiting over there, who would then take the autograph from the kid and go sell it somewhere. This is how observant Pete was. He knew exactly what was going on, even pointing out the guy across the street to us.

-ΞΩΞ-

GLENN SAMPLE:

When they retired my jersey at the University of Cincinnati, they had a ceremony with about five hundred people in attendance, and Pete did the honors of giving the speech on my behalf. He came all the way up from Florida to do that.

For years Pete gave money to the university to help out with the baseball program, because I didn't always have money for recruiting trips and things like that, and what he gave helped.

There also was a ladies group called the Rosy Reds, and they started a fund to support the University of Cincinnati, and this helped support our scholarships.

-ΞΩΞ-

TOMMY HELMS:

Pete did a lot of charitable things that people have never heard about, stuff like bringing some disadvantaged kid or kid with an illness into the clubhouse.

-ΞΩΞ-

HELMS, on what it means to have Rose's friendship:

Pete's not the type of guy who's going to call you every five months to see how you're doing. That's not him. Pete has some friends, but they're not baseball people.

But it wasn't like I didn't spend time with him. We would have breakfast before a practice and lunch afterward, and then we were around each other for the games. We probably spent about eight hours a day together, so it's not like I wasn't still friends with him. I just didn't go out with him after the games.

BOB HOWSAM:

As Pete got better, he became a little harder to get along with.

KAROLYN ROSE, on Pete's spiritual faith, or lack thereof:

As far as I know, Pete has never been baptized. You know, his father didn't like the idea of our getting married in a Catholic church, as my family is Catholic. But we did get married by Monsignor Sherry in Saint William's Church in Price Hill.

The week before Pete and I were to get married, Pete's dad came to our house to talk to me and my mother about who had pressured Pete into marrying me. I said, "Mr. Rose, I never asked Pete to marry me. He asked me to marry him." That was funny.

I don't think Pete's parents practiced any religion, at least none that I was aware of. After Pete's dad died, his mom eventually got remarried to a Catholic man, and she became a Catholic.

During our wedding ceremony, Pete at one point leaned over to me in the church and said, "Are we married yet?" Monsignor Sherry overheard this, and turned to Pete and whispered, "No, Pete, I'll tell you when you're married."

Even though Pete wasn't Catholic, the church allowed us to get married because Pete signed papers saying that our children would be raised Catholic.

I can't remember Pete's ever going to a church service on his own. I go to church every Sunday and always light a candle for Pete and my two kids, too.

JOHN REWWER, *another Western Hills alum:*

Pete told me one time, "You go into the minor leagues and there are women all over the place, all the time, and all they want to do is get hooked up with somebody and that's their ticket to the big time." The way he described it, it sounded an awful lot like the movie *An Officer and a Gentleman*, picking them up out of those little towns.

BILL CONLIN:

One scene I'll never forget is the one at Veterans Stadium on Pete's thirty-eighth birthday, when a Los Angeles Playmate named Christy hired a banner plane to circle the Vet while Pete was on deck and getting ready to bat in the first inning. The message read "Happy 38, Pete. CU in Frisco. Luv Christy." This caused Carol, his fiancée, who was seated behind the dugout, to dash weeping up the aisle. She tried to enter the clubhouse to confront him but with no luck. They didn't let her in, so she stormed home. Christy was waiting at San Francisco International Airport when the Phillies charter landed that night. She must have been something because Pete bought her a Mercedes.

MEL QUEEN:

In 1961 we were playing in Macon, and we traveled in station wagons. I think we had three of them, and we would have to drive through the mountains to get to a lot of the other towns in which we played. We stuffed eight guys into each car—three in the front seat, three in the back, and two all the way back.

This one time it was about three or four o'clock in the morning, and you've got to remember that most station wagons back then had those big luggage racks on top of them. Pete and Tommy Helms were sitting all the way in back, and at one point—while we were driving down the highway at about sixty or seventy miles an hour—Pete climbed out of the back window. Thank God there was a luggage rack on top of that car, for otherwise Pete never would have played in the big leagues.

He climbed across the top of the car from the back to the front. All of a sudden, he slides down on the front windshield, right in the line of sight of the guy driving, one of our older pitchers. I was sitting in the middle of the front seat, and all of a sudden you see Pete's feet. Startled, the guy driving the car slams on the brakes, and that's where the luggage rack saved Pete. He came flying off the top of the car, but was holding onto the rack with one hand. If the rack hadn't been there, Pete would have gone flying off the car and then we would have run over him.

RICHARD HAUCK:

Pete's done a lot of good things for people that you never read about, such as helping kids, but then he has also done a lot of bad things.

I can remember when his son, Pete Jr., was voted the most valuable player for his Oak Hills High School baseball team. We were at the Old-timers honoring that baseball team, and Little Petey gets a call from his dad, who did not come to the banquet. He called in the middle of the banquet and wanted Petey to leave, because he was bringing some guy in from out of town, and he wanted Petey to meet them and take the guy's daughter out.

What kind of father would do that to his kid, when he's being honored at a banquet? Pete has done some things you wish he hadn't done. Zim (Don Zimmer) told me that Major League Baseball offered Pete an out (in 1989), but he wouldn't take it.

I wish Pete the best. I admire him for what he accomplished, but I don't admire him for what he did with his life.

-=◇=-

On the other hand . . . **GLENN SAMPLE:**

I had a couple of big baseball clinics at the University of Cincinnati. Sparky Anderson came up for me, as did Joe Nuxhall, and they were my two main speakers. We had three or four thousand kids and people at these things. That was right when the Big Red Machine was big. Pete came, too, and he did it because he knew me and he liked doing that stuff. There were a whole bunch of other things like that that Pete did and which people never knew about.

-=◇=-

BOB HOWSAM:

One of the things that made Pete so popular was his signing of autographs. In fact, he would sign so many and keep on signing, that finally we put in a rule limiting time for autographs so that the players could have time to focus on the game. So twenty minutes before game time, that was it—time to go back to the clubhouse to change shirts and think about the game coming up.

KAROLYN ROSE, *on her son, Pete Jr.:*

I think that my son, Pete, would also be in the big leagues today if it hadn't been for all this. I think Cincinnati gave him a dirty deal because of (manager) Jack McKeon. Petey had a really good year down in Nashville, and they brought him up at the end of the year. My biggest thrill in my entire life, and I say this from the bottom of my heart, was when he came on that field and was wearing his dad's uniform number fourteen.

They had one last road trip at the end of the season, for four days I think it was, and McKeon told Pete that he would be playing the last three days. Well, he didn't put him in until the seventh inning of the last game. After the game, McKeon went on TV and talked about all his rookies and never said anything about Pete. That hurts.

When Pete Sr. was playing, I didn't care when anyone said anything about him, because I knew it didn't bother him. But throwing stuff at him was another story. He could get hurt and have his career ruined.

It's different with Pete Jr. When he got into (minor-league) baseball, he was once playing a game in Frederick, Maryland. I'm sitting in the stands of this small ballpark, and these two fellows, half-loaded, come over and sit down about five rows from me. When Pete got up to bat, these two guys started right in with Pete.

"Heyyyyy, Petey, have you got a bet on this time?" Blah, blah-blah, blah-blah. This went on for a while. Next time Petey comes up, one of the guys yells out, "You stink just like your daddy! Do you have a bet on? Did you pay your taxes?"

At that point I couldn't hold it in anymore. I yelled down at these guys "Excuse me, numbnuts!" This one guy making most of the noise turns around and looks at me: "Are you talking to me?" I said, "I guess so, because you answered, numbnuts."

"You gotta problem, lady?"

"I don't have the problem. You have the problem. You have two things you can do. You take your best shot at me or you hit the pavement, pal."

The other guy then looks back, sees me, and says, "Oh, geez. That's Pete Rose's mom. Don't you read the paper, man? She goes after people and can really fight."

"Oh, Mrs. Rose, I'm sorry," this other guy says. "My friend is really drunk and doesn't know what he's saying. I'm going to take him home now." And they got up and left.

They were getting on my baby. Big mistake.

⊏◊⊐

KAROLYN, on Petey:

He looks exactly like his father, but he has my personality. He recently did a television piece in which he said, "My sister can play ball better than me." And Fawn is a good player.

⊏◊⊐

KAROLYN ROSE, on Pete Sr. as a dad:

Fawny is very personal. She's not in the limelight, and she never was. So many people over the years have told me they didn't realize I also had a daughter. That's because when Pete talked about his family, it was always about Petey. That hurts you.

Pete Sr. is getting older, and there will come a day when he suddenly realizes how much he has missed. He won't know until he hits seventy how much he missed with our kids. But I'm thankful that neither of my children have gotten into trouble. Fawn would tell me how people would come up to her and ask her if she wanted anything, like some grass or uppers. She told me she could have gotten anything she wanted because the people who had the stuff assured her that her dad had plenty of money and that she could get anything at any time.

When she told me this, I asked her, "Well, what did you tell them?"

She said, "No thanks, and I went on."

I raised both our kids, and I raised them to never hate their father. "You've got only one father and one mother. You respect them." Even the Bible says that.

⚬

BILL CONLIN:

When Pete was playing with the Phils, he lived about a mile and a half from me in an area about twelve miles outside Philadelphia called the townships, just over in New Jersey.

I remember one time in the summer when my son and three of his American Legion teammates were out one day throwing batting practice to each other at a community batting cage. It was about a hundred degrees, and all of a sudden Pete comes roaring up in his red Porsche. He recognizes my son and his pals, and he gets out of his car wearing this red-velour suit.

First thing you know, Pete is in the batting cage with them, giving them this incredible seminar on hitting that goes on for fifteen minutes, then thirty, then forty-five, and then he changes the subject to the proper bunting technique. By then, Pete is sweating like a pig but doing this with such zeal. It's the damnedest thing. And I'll tell you what, all four of those guys went on to play Division I college ball, and each was the best bunter on his respective team.

This was where Pete's love for the game shined through in a circumstance where there's no money in it for him.

MEL QUEEN:

Pete Rose was extraordinary in every game you watched. On offense. Defense? He was a little shaky, but because of his drive and determination, he became a good defensive player even though he did not have good defensive ability.

The one thing I remember him telling me: "Queenie, I'm going to be the first $100,000-a-year singles hitter." The guys making a hundred grand back then were the home-run hitters, as well as (Sandy) Koufax and (Don) Drysdale.

QUEEN, *talking about his days as an outfielder before*
he switched over to pitching:

Another story about Pete concerns my first base hit in the major leagues. I'm pinch hitting and Mr. Juan Marichal is pitching (for the San Francisco Giants). I'm in the on-deck circle swinging a bat, and Pete comes up and says, "Queenie, be ready, he's going to challenge you. He'll challenge you."

So I go up there looking for a Sandy Koufax or Don Wilson-type fastball. But he throws me one of those friggin' screwballs of his. I started to swing and then tried to hold up, pulled my bat back, hit myself in the head, knocking my helmet off, and I had to go over and pick it up near the on-deck circle. There's Pete, and I tell him, "Hey, Pete, so much for challenging somebody, huh?" And he goes, "Queenie, he's going to throw you a fastball. Be ready."

So a couple of pitches later I get the fastball, and I ground one through the infield, up the middle, for a single, my first major-league hit. It felt pretty good.

KAROLYN ROSE:

Pete and Eddie Brinkman were good friends. One year when Pete had made the National League All-Star team, Eddie was over at the house visiting, and Pete spent much of the time asking Eddie about the American League pitchers he might be facing, trying to get a handle on how they might pitch to him.

If I remember, Pete struck out first time up in the game. Later, after the season, Pete runs into Eddie and says, "Eddie, what the hell's wrong with you? You told me about this one particular guy, that he likes to throw a slider. Well, he threw me a fastball!"

TIM SULLIVAN:

The last time I saw Pete was two summers ago (2001) in Cooperstown, where I was covering the induction ceremony. I was staying in a hotel that had two floors, which is pretty rare in Cooperstown. As I was about to check out that Monday morning, I looked over this balcony and saw Pete sitting over in a corner of this big lobby.

I held up my hand and gave him a little half-wave, and I'm pretty sure we made eye contact. I can't be absolutely sure. But by the time I had gotten on the elevator and gone down to the first-floor lobby, Pete had left the lobby—at a dead run, it appeared. So I guess I can assume that I'm not on his Christmas-card list at this point.

When I left Cincinnati in May 2002 to move to San Diego, part of my last column dealt with what had happened to Pete and my love-hate relationship with him. As much as I admired what he represented in baseball, I felt like somebody still needed to talk tough to him, to tell him that what he needed to do was straighten up his act. I thought that fell in part to me, at least in that town.

If you love baseball and want to find a happy ending for Pete, he still has to come clean. A lot of all this could have been avoided if he had done this about fifteen years ago.

BILL CONLIN:

Of all the baseball people I've covered in thirty-seven years, Pete Rose is head and shoulders the most fascinating of all of them. He was the best interview, the best quote machine, and the most relentlessly driven player I've ever seen. That was evident the time when he started raging at the light when Paul Owens benched him for Game Five of the 1983 World Series. That was the clue that Pete wouldn't be coming back to the Phils in 1984 and that the gambling genie was out of the bottle.

KAROLYN ROSE, *on the theory that behind every successful man resides a good woman:*

I could never take any credit for anything he did on the field. I think I can take a little bit of credit for doing what I could to protect his image as a father and a husband.

TOMMY HELMS:

He's still the most popular athlete in the Cincinnati area.

10

RE-PETE

For more than twenty-five years, Pete Rose put a lot of deposits in his bank with writers who would someday be casting Hall of Fame ballots with his name on them. Writers by the dozens not only sought out Rose, he sought them out as well. And he almost always delivered the goods, Jim Gray notwithstanding.

Rose has to rank as one of the most accessible and most quotable sports figures of all time, right up there with the likes of Magic Johnson, Charles Barkley, and Bobby Bowden. When a writer was on a postgame deadline crunch and needed a couple of quick quotes before dashing back to the press box to file a story, Rose was the go-to guy, win or lose. Even if you were critical of him, Rose would still face you the next day and answer your next round of questions.

In May 1985, only about an hour before game time at the Houston Astrodome, Rose, then the Reds' player-manager, granted a forty-minute interview to a *Fort Worth Star-Telegram* sports reporter he had never met before.

Rose was closing in on Ty Cobb's career hit record, and he had a team in contention, but once the door to his office closed, he was totally focused on the interview, answering questions thoughtfully and, rapid-fire, providing statistical trivia relevant to the story. The only drawback was Rose's use of profanity, so incessant at times that it became a distraction.

⊏◌⊐

On Cincinnati:

I was raised here, but I never did grow up.[1]

⊏◌⊐

On his love of baseball:

I'd walk through hell in a gasoline suit to keep playing baseball.[2]

⊏◌⊐

On his intelligence:

I'm living proof that you don't have to be smart to make a lot of money.[3]

⊏◌⊐

On being a manager:

I'm unorthodox, but I get the job done.[4]

I try to create a relaxed atmosphere in the clubhouse so everybody can have fun.[5]

On winning and losing:

You never take losing in stride. If you tell me the Reds are going to win a hundred games this year, I'd be as happy as a pig in slop. Yet that means we're going to lose sixty-two. What you try to do is get your team to lose just the games you're supposed to lose.[6]

On his work ethic:

Everything I've achieved in this game is from dedication and hard work.[7]

On the difficulty of getting four thousand hits in a career:

The first three thousands hits is easy. It's the next thousand that's tough.[8]

On Joe DiMaggio:

I played in more wins than DiMaggio played games.[9]

On the night he got his two thousandth hit:

Took Cobb this long to get to 1,861.[10]

✦

On his scuffle with Bud Harrelson:

I made him a star.[11]

✦

On staying away from gambling, spoken about ten years after Rose was banned from baseball by then-Major League Baseball Commissioner Bart Giamatti:

Bart Giamatti told me to reconfigure my life, and I have. I don't gamble illegally. I'm real careful who I associate with.[12]

✦

On negotiating his settlement with Giamatti regarding his banishment:

During our negotiations they said it'd be twenty-two years till I could apply for reinstatement. We got it down to eleven, then to one year, and that's when I signed.[13]

✦

Speaking on the eve of the launch of his Hall of Fame Induction Petition at Sportcut.com:

Sure, I'd love to be in the Hall of Fame, but I'm a baseball person. I'm a teacher. I want to get back on the field. I don't care how many restaurants or how many radio shows you have. To make the kind of money managers are making now—and I'd be right up there with my credentials—it's a hell of a job.[14]

✦

On the long years of no response to his appeals for
lifting the ban:

Even Charles Manson gets a hearing every two years. My
son thinks I'm a monster.[15]

⊏◇⊐

On being challenged by NBC's Jim Gray before Game Two
of the '99 World Series to repent of his alleged gambling:

This is a prosecutor's brief, not an interview, and I'm very
surprised at you.[16]

⊏◇⊐

On being hired by Maaco to be the company's celebrity
spokesman, his first national endorsement deal since
being banned from baseball in 1989:

Corporate America's letting me back in. The Maaco door is
going to open other doors.[17]

⊏◇⊐

On his banishment from the game he loves:

It's a sad scenario in my case, but I would have been a lot better off had I been addicted to drugs as opposed to betting on
football. (He refuses to admit he bet on baseball.) I wouldn't
be here right now. If I was manager for the Reds, they would
have paid for my rehab. It's sad to say, but that's the truth.[18]

⊏◇⊐

On bookies:

The majority of bookmakers are crybabies. You know, they
could have the biggest weekend in the world, and they're

always complaining about the losses. In reality . . . no book-makers lose.[19]

Reflecting on some of his most significant statistical accomplishments:

The three most important things to me were hits, wins, and runs scored. I finished first in hits, won more games than any-body, and was second in runs. Two out of three ain't bad.[20]

In a written statement upon submitting his guilty plea in federal court on tax-evasion charges:

I'm asked a lot about the Hall of Fame. There's no question that my baseball records earned me a place, but I understand that the Hall of Fame means more than 4,256 hits.[21]

A PETE ROSE TIMELINE

HIGHLIGHTS OF CHARLIE HUSTLE'S MAJOR LEAGUE BASEBALL CAREER

1963

March 10: As a non-roster player, Pete Rose makes his first appearance with the Reds, entering a spring game against the Chicago White Sox in the ninth inning. He doubles in both the eleventh and fourteenth innings and scores the game's only run.

April 9: Rose walks in his first official major-league plate appearance as the Reds beat the Pittsburgh Pirates, 5–2.

May 3: Rose hits first major-league home run, off Ernie Broglio of the Saint Louis Cardinals, as the Reds win, 6–0.

November 26: Rose wins the National League's Rookie of the Year Award, garnering seventeen of twenty votes.

1964

April 23: A ninth-inning error allows Rose to score the winning run in 1–0 victory over the Astros, as Houston's Ken Johnson becomes first pitcher to toss a nine-inning no-hitter and lose.

October 2: With first place in the National League on the line, a routine infield flyball drops between Rose and shortstop Leo Cardenas. That opens the way for the Phillies to rally for four runs and beat the Reds, 4–3.

Source: BaseballLibrary.com

1966

August 30: Rose becomes the twelfth player in major-league history to hit home runs from both sides of the plate, as the Reds beat the Cardinals, 6–4.

1968

September 28: Rose goes 5–for–5 against Gaylord Perry in 10–4 loss to the San Francisco Giants as he battles down to the wire against Matty Alou of the Chicago Cubs for the National League batting crown.

September 29: Pete Rose goes 1–for–3 to wrap up the batting title over Alou, .335 to .332.

November 18: Rose finishes second to Bob Gibson of the Cardinals in the National League MVP voting.

1969

April 7: Rose and Bobby Tolan lead off the home half of the season opener with back-to-back home runs against Don Drysdale, but the Los Angeles Dodgers prevail, 3–2. Rose and Tolan would end up doing this nine times.

June 9: Rose, Jim Maloney, and Tommy Helms defy a team vote to boycott the game against the Chicago Cubs after President Lyndon Johnson declares a national day of mourning following the assassination of Robert Kennedy. Those three Reds leave the clubhouse for the field, and the rest of the team follows. The Reds beat the Cubs, 4–1.

October 2: On the last day of season, Rose is .0008 ahead of the Pirates' Roberto Clemente in the National League batting race and locks up the title, at .348, with a drag-bunt single in his last at-bat in an 8–3 victory at Atlanta.

October 9: Sparky Anderson is hired to replace Dave Bristol as Cincinnati manager. Another piece of the Big Red Machine falls into place.

1970

February 28: Rose signs a new contract for an estimated $105,000 a year, fulfilling his stated goal to become baseball's first $100,000 singles hitter.

July 14: Rose barrels into catcher Ray Fosse in a home-plate collision to score from second on Jim Hickman's twelfth-inning single, giving the National League a 5–4 victory at Riverfront Stadium in the 41st All-Star Game.

1972

May 16: Rose knocks in the winning run in 4–3 victory over the San Francisco Giants by spoiling pitcher Ron Bryant's attempted intentional walk. Bryant's fourth pitch comes close enough for Rose to go after the pitch and reach base on an error that allows the winning run to score.

1973

June 19: Rose singles in a 4–0 victory over the Giants for his 2,000th career

hit. Willie Davis of the Dodgers gets his 2,000th hit on same day.

October 8: Rose tussles at second base with the Mets' Bud Harrelson and gets the TKO, although the Mets get in last shot, a 9–2 victory that gives them a 2–1 lead in the National League Championship Series.

November 21: Pete Rose wins the National League MVP Award, barely beating out Willie Stargell of the Pirates. Rose led the league with 230 hits and won his third batting crown, at .338.

1974

April 4: Rose scores from second on a Buzz Capra wild pitch in the eleventh inning for a 7–6 victory over the Braves, in the same game in which Hank Aaron, on his first swing of the season, ties Babe Ruth with his 714th career home run.

1975

May 3: Rose accepts a switch from left field to third base, opening up a lineup spot for outfield prospect George Foster, who would go on to average 36 homers, 117 RBIs, and .302 over the next four seasons.

August 17: Rose gets his 2,500th career hit, off Pittsburgh's Bruce Kison, in a 3–1 Reds victory over the Pirates.

October 22: Rose is named World Series MVP after the Reds win the Series over the Boston Red Sox by eking out a 4–3 win in Game Seven.

1977

May 7: Rose has two hits in 12–10 loss to the Pirates at Three Rivers

Stadium, running his hitting streak to twenty games. He would go hitless the next day but would piece together another twenty-game hitting streak later in the season.

July 25: Rose singles off Pete Falcone in a 9–8 loss to the Cardinals for his 2,881st career hit, surpassing Frankie Frisch for the all-time hits lead among switch-hitters.

1978

May 5: Rose singles off of Montreal's Steve Rogers for his 3,000th hit and gets a hug at first base from former teammate Tony Perez, now with the Expos.

May 7: Stomach cramps force Rose to sit out the nightcap of a double-header at Riverfront against Montreal, ending his consecutive game-playing streak at 678.

June 13: Rose goes hitless in the Reds' 1–0 victory over the Cubs, dipping his average to .267 during a 5-for-44 slump. It will be August before he again goes hitless.

July 24: Two singles against the Mets extend Rose's new hitting streak to thirty-seven games, tying him for the modern-day National League record held by Tommy Holmes.

July 31: Rose singles off Phil Niekro of the Braves to extend his hitting streak to forty-four games, tying the NL's all-time record set by Willie Keeler in 1897, when foul balls didn't count as strikes.

August 1: Pitchers Larry McWilliams and Gene Garber of the Braves combine to hold Rose hitless in a 16–4 Braves win at Atlanta, ending Rose's streak at forty-four games.

October 1: Rose, with 198 hits, is deprived of the 200-hit mark for the season when manager Sparky Anderson removes him from a game against the Braves.

December 5: Rose signs a four-year, $3.2 million contract with the Phillies, temporarily making him highest-paid player in team sports.

1979

August 5: Rose gets his 2,427th career single, breaking Honus Wagner's National League record, as the Phillies lose to the Pirates.

September 24: Rose singles in a 7–2 loss to the Saint Louis Cardinals, giving him 200 hits in a season for the tenth time, breaking the former record of nine held by Ty Cobb. The hit extends Rose's hitting streak to eighteen games, and it would eventually reach twenty-three by season's end.

1980

May 11: Living up to his Charlie Hustle nickname, Rose steals second, third, and home in the same inning against the Reds in Cincinnati, becoming the first National Leaguer to pull off that feat since Jackie Robinson twenty-six years earlier. The Phils win, 7–3.

June 13: Rose goes 4-for-5 in a 9–6 Philadelphia win over the San Diego Padres and moves past Honus Wagner on the all-time hits list with 3,431.

1981

June 10: Rose singles off Nolan Ryan in the first inning of 5–4 Phillies victory over the Astros to tie Stan

Musial for second place on National League career hits list, with 3,630. He strikes out in his next three at-bats. This is the last game before a major-league work stoppage, meaning Rose will have to wait to pass Musial.

August 10: After a two-month wait, Rose finally breaks Stan Musial's National League hits record by hitting a single off Saint Louis's Mark Littell.

1982

June 20: A 3–1 loss to the Pirates at Three Rivers Stadium is Rose's 3,000th career game, putting him in elite group that also includes Ty Cobb, Stan Musial, Hank Aaron, and Carl Yastrzemski.

June 22: Rose's third-inning double in a 3–2 loss to the Cardinals is his 3,772nd hit, moving him past Hank Aaron as the National League career hits leader.

1983

August 24: Rose sits out a 5–3 loss to the Giants, ending his consecutive-games streak at 745.

December 22: Rose wins his lawsuit against the IRS and is awarded a $36,083 tax refund from 1978.

1984

January 20: About to turn forty-three, Rose signs a one-year contract with the Montreal Expos.

April 13: Rose doubles off Jerry Koosman to collect his 4,000th career hit in 5–1 victory over the Phils.

June 29: Rose plays in his 3,309th game, passing Carl Yastrzemski as Major League Baseball's all-time

leader in games played. The Expos beat the Reds, 7–3, at Riverfront.

July 27: In a 6–1 victory over the Phils, Rose hits his 3,053rd career single, this one off Steve Carlton, moving him past Ty Cobb for the all-time singles lead.

August 15: Pete Rose is traded back to the Reds for infielder Tom Lawless and is immediately named player-manager to replace the deposed Vern Rapp.

August 17: In first game back in a Reds uniform, Rose and the Reds beat the Cubs, 6–4, at Riverfront.

1985

September 8: Rose catches Cobb at 4,191 career hits with a base hit at Wrigley Field off Chicago's Reggie Patterson.

September 11: Rose singles off San Diego's Eric Show in first inning of 2–0 Reds win for hit number 4,192. An emotional Rose looks up in sky a la Luke Skywalker and sees his dad and Ty Cobb looking down on him.

1986

August 17: Rose makes his final major-league appearance as a player, striking out as a pinch hitter against Goose Gossage as the Reds lose, 9–5, to the San Diego Padres.

November 11: Pete Rose is dropped from the Reds' forty-man roster to make room for pitcher Pat Pacillo.

1987

May 1: Cincinnati beats Philadelphia, 8–5, to climb into first place for first time after April under Rose.

August 4: A 2–1 loss to the Cardinals at Riverfront begins a seven-game losing streak that drops the Reds out of first, never to return. But the team wins seven of its last eight games of the season to finish in second place, six games back.

1988

May 2: National League President Bart Giamatti suspends Pete Rose for thirty days following an incident two days earlier in which Rose shoved umpire Dave Pallone in a 6–5 loss to the Mets at Riverfront.

1989

February 21: Rose meets with Major League Baseball Commissioner Peter Ueberroth and Commissioner-elect Bart Giamatti to discuss Rose's purported gambling habits, which Rose downplays.

March 20: The commissioner's office announces that Rose is under investigation for unnamed "serious allegations."

August 24: Giamatti permanently bans Rose from baseball for his alleged gambling on Major League Baseball games.

1990

April 20: Rose pleads guilty to two felony counts of filing false income tax returns.

July 19: Rose is sentenced to five months in prison and fined $50,000 for tax evasion.

August 8: Rose begins serving his five-month sentence at Marion Federal Prison Camp in Illinois.

1991

January 7: Released from federal prison, Rose begins 1,000 hours of community service.

February 4: The Baseball Hall of Fame's twelve-man board of directors votes unanimously to bar Pete Rose from the ballot. He will become eligible again only if the commissioner reinstates him by December 2005.

1992

January 7: In what would have been Rose's first year of Hall of Fame eligibility, pitchers Tom Seaver and Rollie Fingers are elected. Rose receives forty-one write-in votes.

1998

November 13: Among the items auctioned off at a baseball memorabilia auction is the bat Rose used to get his record-breaking 4,192nd hit. It is sold for $21,096.

1999

August 23: Commissioner Bud Selig announces that a ban exception will be made, allowing Rose to participate in a World Series ceremony if he is elected to the All-Century Team, which he is.

November 30: Rose launches a new Web site, where fans can go to add their names to a petition for his reinstatement to baseball.

2001

August 6: Former Rose acquaintance Tommy Gioiosa alleges in a *Vanity Fair* interview that Rose had bet on baseball, used a corked bat, and participated in drug dealing.

PETE ROSE'S CAREER RECORD

Year	Team	G	AB	R	H	2B	3B	HR	RBI	SB	BA	OBP
1963	Reds	157	623	101	170	25	9	6	41	13	.273	.334
1964	Reds	136	516	64	139	13	2	4	34	4	.269	.319
1965	Reds	162	670	117	209	35	11	11	81	8	.312	.382
1966	Reds	156	654	97	205	38	5	16	70	4	.313	.351
1967	Reds	148	585	86	176	32	8	12	76	11	.301	.364
1968	Reds	149	626	94	210	42	6	10	49	3	.335	.391
1969	Reds	156	627	120	218	33	11	16	82	7	.348	.428
1970	Reds	159	649	120	205	37	9	15	52	12	.316	.385
1971	Reds	160	632	86	192	27	4	13	44	13	.304	.373
1972	Reds	154	645	107	198	31	11	6	57	10	.307	.382
1973	Reds	160	680	115	230	38	8	5	64	10	.338	.401
1974	Reds	163	652	110	185	45	7	3	51	2	.284	.385
1975	Reds	162	662	112	210	47	4	7	74	0	.317	.406
1976	Reds	162	665	130	215	42	6	10	63	9	.323	.404
1977	Reds	162	655	95	204	38	7	9	64	16	.311	.377
1978	Reds	159	655	103	198	51	3	7	52	13	.302	.362
1979	Phils	163	628	90	208	40	5	4	59	20	.331	.418
1980	Phils	162	655	95	185	42	1	1	64	12	.282	.352
1981	Phils	107	431	73	140	18	5	0	33	4	.325	.391
1982	Phils	162	634	80	172	25	4	3	54	8	.271	.345
1983	Phils	151	493	52	121	14	3	0	45	7	.245	.316
1984	Expos-											
	Reds	121	374	43	107	15	2	0	34	1	.286	.359
1985	Reds	119	405	60	107	12	2	2	46	8	.264	.319
1986	Reds	72	237	15	52	8	2	0	25	3	.219	.316
Totals		3,562	14,053	2,165	4,256	746	135	160	1,314	198	.303	.375

Source: CBSSportsline.com and Baseball-Reference.com

PETE ROSE'S
KEY ACHIEVEMENTS

Major League Awards

1963 National League Rookie of the Year
1968 National League Batting Champion
1969 National League Batting Champion
1969 National League Gold Glove Award
1970 National League Gold Glove Award
1973 National League Most Valuable Player
1973 National League Batting Champion
1975 World Series Most Valuable Player

Major League Records

Career Hits	4,256
Games Played	3,562
At-Bats	14,053
Singles	3,315
Total Bases by Switch-Hitter	5,752
Seasons of 200 or More Hits	10
Consecutive Seasons of 100 or More Hits	23
Seasons With 600 or More At-Bats	17
Seasons With 150 or More Games Played	17
Seasons With 100 or More Games Played	23
Most Winning Games Played In	1,972

National League Records

Most Years Played	24
Most Consecutive Years Played	24
Career Runs	2,165
Career Doubles	746
Most Games With Five or More Hits	10
Consecutive Game Hitting Streak	44
Most Consecutive Game Hitting Streaks of 20 or More Games	7

Pete Rose is the only player in major-league history to play at least 500 games at five different positions: first base (939), second base (628), third base (634), left field (671), and right field (595).

NOTES

Chapter 1: Pee Wee Petey

1. Rose, Pete, and Roger Kahn, *Pete Rose: My Story*. New York: Macmillan, 1989, 75.

2. Reston, James Jr., *Collision at Home Plate*. Lincoln, NE: University of Nebraska Press, 1991, 10.

3. Rose, Pete, and Roger Kahn, *Pete Rose: My Story*, 77.

4. Sokolove, Michael Y., *Hustle: The Myth, Life, and Lies of Pete Rose*. New York: Simon and Schuster, 1990, 3.

5. Rose, Pete, and Roger Kahn, *Pete Rose: My Story*, 80.

6. Rose, Pete, and Roger Kahn, *Pete Rose: My Story*, 72–72.

7. Sokolove, Michael Y., *Hustle: The Myth, Life, and Lies of Pete Rose*, 35.

8. Sokolove, Michael Y., Hustle: *The Myth, Life, and Lies of Pete Rose*, 36.

9. Rose, Pete, and Roger Kahn, *Pete Rose: My Story*, 79–80.

10. Sokolove, Michael Y., Hustle: *The Myth, Life, and Lies of Pete Rose*, 28.

Chapter 2: Charlie Hustle

1. Will, George F., *Bunts*, from a June 29, 1991, column entitled "The Collision Between Bart and Pete." New York: Scribner, 1998, 196.

2. Rose, Pete, and Roger Kahn, *Pete Rose: My Story*. New York: Macmillan, 1989, 92.

3. Reston, James Jr., *Collision at Home Plate*. Lincoln, NE: University of Nebraska Press, 1991, 36.

4. Rose, Pete, and Roger Kahn, *Pete Rose: My Story*, 96.

5. Rose, Pete, and Roger Kahn, *Pete Rose: My Story*, 97.

6. Rose, Pete, and Roger Kahn, *Pete Rose: My Story*, 9.

7. Reston, James Jr., *Collision at Home Plate*, 45–46.

8. Sokolove, Michael Y., *Hustle: The Myth, Life, and Lies of Pete Rose*. New York: Simon and Schuster, 1990, 57.

9. Sokolove, Michael Y., *Hustle: The Myth, Life, and Lies of Pete Rose*, 57.

10. Rose, Pete, and Roger Kahn, *Pete Rose: My Story*, 110.

11. Rose, Pete, and Roger Kahn, *Pete Rose: My Story*, 147.

12. Sokolove, Michael Y., Hustle: *The Myth, Life, and Lies of Pete Rose*, 71.

13. Rose, Pete, and Roger Kahn, *Pete Rose: My Story*, 134–35.

14. Reston, James Jr., *Collision at Home Plate*, 66–67.

15. Sokolove, Michael Y., Hustle: *The Myth, Life, and Lies of Pete Rose*, 184.

Chapter 3: The Big Red Machine
1. *The Sporting News*, Oct. 7, 2002.
2. Rose, Pete, and Roger Kahn, *Pete Rose: My Story*. New York: Macmillan, 1989, 175.
3. Rose, Pete, and Roger Kahn, *Pete Rose: My Story*. New York: Macmillan, 1989, 198.
4. Rose, Pete, and Roger Kahn, *Pete Rose: My Story*. New York: Macmillan, 1989, 198.

Chapter 4: Fill 'er Up
1. Sokolove, Michael Y., *Hustle: The Myth, Life, and Lies of Pete Rose*. New York: Simon and Schuster, 1990, 214–215.

Chapter 5: Home Again
1. Rose, Pete, and Roger Kahn, *Pete Rose: My Story*. New York: Macmillan, 1989, 32.
2. Sokolove, Michael Y., *Hustle: The Myth, Life, and Lies of Pete Rose*. New York: Simon and Schuster, 1990, 108.

Chapter 6: Chasing Ty Cobb
1. *Baseball Digest*, November 1999.
2. Sokolove, Michael Y., *Hustle: The Myth, Life, and Lies of Pete Rose*. New York: Simon and Schuster, 1990, 118.
3. Reston, James Jr., *Collision at Home Plate*. Lincoln, NE: University of Nebraska Press, 1991, 195.
4. *Baseball Digest*, November 1999.

Chapter 7: Go Down Gambling
1. Sokolove, Michael Y., *Hustle: The Myth, Life, and Lies of Pete Rose*. New York: Simon and Schuster, 1990, 255.
2. *Penthouse*, September 1990.
3. Sokolove, Michael Y., *Hustle: The Myth, Life, and Lies of Pete Rose*. New York: Simon and Schuster, 1990, 222.
4. Morgan, Joe, with Richard Lally, *Long Balls, No Strikes*. New York: Random House, 1999, 163.
5. *USA Today*, March 10, 2003.
6. www.baseball1.com
7. Sokolove, Michael Y., *Hustle: The Myth, Life, and Lies of Pete Rose*. New York: Simon and Schuster, 1990, 293
8. James, Bill, *The Politics of Glory*. New York: Macmillan, 1994, 357–58.

Chapter 8: "C," for Cooperstown
1. Morgan, Joe, with Richard Lally, *Long Balls, No Strikes*. New York: Random House, 1999, 165–66.
2. USA Today, March 10, 2003.
3. James, Bill, The Politics of Glory. New York: Macmillan, 1994, 356–57.

Chapter 9: Rose Redux
1. Will, George F., *Bunts*. New York: Scribner, 1998, 199.

5. Sokolove, Michael Y., *Hustle: The Myth, Life, and Lies of Pete Rose*. New York: Simon and Schuster, 1990, 165.

2. Sokolove, Michael Y., *Hustle: The Myth, Life, and Lies of Pete Rose*. New York: Simon and Schuster, 1990, 275–76.

3. Will, George F., *Bunts*. New York: Scribner, 1998, 119.

Chapter 10: Re-Pete

1. Reston, James Jr., *Collision at Home Plate*. Lincoln, NE: University of Nebraska Press, 1991, 142.

2. BaseballLibrary.com

3. Reston, James Jr., *Collision at Home Plate*. Lincoln, NE: University of Nebraska Press, 1991, 142.

4. *Fort Worth Star-Telegram*, May 6, 1985.

5. Sokolove, Michael Y., *Hustle: The Myth, Life, and Lies of Pete Rose*. New York: Simon and Schuster, 1990, 217.

6. *Fort Worth Star-Telegram*, May 6, 1985.

7. *Fort Worth Star-Telegram*, May 6, 1985.

8. *Sports Illustrated*, Aug. 16, 1999.

9. *The Sporting News*, Dec. 13, 1999.

10. *The Sporting News*, Dec. 13, 1999.

11. Reston, James Jr., *Collision at Home Plate*. Lincoln, NE: University of Nebraska Press, 1991, 142.

12. *Sports Illustrated*, Aug. 16, 1999.

13. *Sports Illustrated*, Aug. 16, 1999.

14. *Sports Illustrated*, Dec. 6, 1999.

15. *Newsweek*, Dec. 13, 1999.

16. *Public Relations Tactics*, January 2000.

17. *Sports Illustrated*, July 31, 2000.

18. BaseballLibrary.com.

19. BaseballLibrary.com.

20. BaseballLibrary.com.

21. Sokolove, Michael Y., *Hustle: The Myth, Life, and Lies of Pete Rose*. New York: Simon and Schuster, 1990, 289.

INDEX

Printed in the USA
CPSIA information can be obtained
at www.ICGtesting.com
JSHW082200140824
68134JS00014B/342